ABOUT THE AUTHORS

Richard Reeves is a Senior Fellow at the Brookings Institution in Washington DC. He also teaches at Georgetown University. Before moving to the United States in 2012, he worked as Director of Strategy to the UK's Deputy Prime Minister, Nick Clegg. Richard's previous roles include Director of Demos, the London-based political think tank; Editor-at-large and columnist for *Management Today*; Society Editor of the *Observer*; Economics Correspondent of the *Guardian*; and Research Fellow at the Institute for Public Policy Research.

John Knell is one of the UK's leading thinkers on the changing face of work and organizations, and as a strategy consultant works widely across the private, public and third sectors. Over the last ten years he has built an international reputation as a cultural policy analyst, working with governments, funders, cities and major cultural institutions around the world. He has also been developing the Culture Counts platform (www.culturecounts.cc) to support the use of the quality metrics he has helped co-produce with the cultural sector in Australia and the United Kingdom. He was previously Director of Research and Advocacy at The Work Foundation, where he played a key role in transforming the organization into an authority on work issues. He has authored numerous reports on work, organizational change and public policy.

THE
80 MINUTE MBA

Everything You'll Never Learn at Business School

The fully revised new edition
of the international bestseller

Richard Reeves
and
John Knell

NICHOLAS BREALEY
PUBLISHING

London · Boston

New edition first published in 2017 by Nicholas Brealey Publishing
An imprint of John Murray Press
An Hachette UK Company

This paperback edition published in 2019 by Nicholas Brealey Publishing

First published in 2009 by Headline Publishing Group

1

A CIP catalogue record for this title is available from the British Library

ISBN 978-1-473-69609-9
Ebook ISBN UK 978-0-755-36491-6
Ebook ISBN US 978-1-473-67870-5

Typeset in Century by
Palimpsest Book Production Ltd, Falkirk, Stirlingshire

Printed and bound by Clays Ltd, Elcograf S.p.A.

Nicholas Brealey policy is to use papers that are natural, renewable
and recyclable products and made from wood grown in sustainable forests.
The logging and manufacturing processes are expected to conform to the
environmental regulations of the country of origin.

Nicholas Brealey Publishing
John Murray Press
Carmelite House
50 Victoria Embankment
London EC4Y 0DZ
Tel: 020 3122 6000

Nicholas Brealey Publishing
Hachette Book Group
Market Place Center, 53 State Street
Boston, MA 02109, USA
Tel: (617) 263 1834

www.nicholasbrealey.com
www.the80minutemba.com

DEDICATION

This book is dedicated to all those who refuse
to see business education as an oxymoron.

ACKNOWLEDGEMENTS

We'd like to thank the man who helped us put *The 80 Minute MBA* into the market, Brendan Barnes from the London Business Forum. The numerous clients with whom we have worked, and from whom we have learned so much. Our agent, Toby Mundy. And last but not least, Holly Bennion from John Murray Press, who has provided the perfect balance of what policy wonks call 'help and hassle' in order to produce this new edition.

CONTENTS

CITIUS EST MELIUS

(Quicker is better)

INTRODUCTION

You're busy, we know. Too busy to read many of the thousands of business books published each year. Perhaps too busy to attend very many 'professional development' courses. And certainly too pressed to take a year or two out to do an MBA course. You may in any case be sceptical of how much you can really learn from the gurus, professors and corporate titans who line up to proffer their advice.

We're with you. Business courses and books can, of course, be enlightening and inspiring. But more often they are a mixture of the blindingly obvious and wildly utopian. In the years we've been researching and advising on organizational issues, we've realized the value of simply cutting to the chase. No throat-clearing, winding anecdotes or lengthy case studies: just the key insights and killer facts.

This book contains the distillate of an MBA course. Just as the creators of the Reduced Shakespeare Company brought the works of the Bard to the stage in shortened format, so we have attempted to bring the best of business thinking into a single, slim volume, drawing on a presentation of the same name which we have been delivering over the last ten years. *The 80 Minute MBA* should do what it says on the tin. So if you read slightly quicker than the average person (and we know you do) this book should only take an hour and twenty minutes to read. Like all self-respecting MBA courses, ours has a motto: *citius est melius* – quicker is better.

We've had a good time synthesizing the material – remembering Noël Coward reckoned that work was 'more fun than fun' – and hope that comes across in what follows. But we are deadly serious about the potential of organizations and their leaders to create better work, more economic value and stronger human relationships. We can be sceptical, but, we hope, never cynical. An irreducible core of optimism runs through our work. Business life can be – should be – good.

But it is also clear that we are writing against dark skies. The 2008 global financial crisis continues to cast a long shadow. Businesses and governments alike have seen their reputations battered. Public trust in the major institutions of government, business, media and NGOs has hit rock bottom around the globe. The credibility of CEOs dropped to an all-time low of 37% in a recent study, and is plummeting in every country studied. Business leaders are now only 8% above political leaders (29%) in terms of public trust. For those in or seeking leadership positions in business life, the scale of the challenge is clear.[1]

You don't have to be an Eeyore to see the size of the deficits confronting us. Our compressed MBA is constructed in clear sight of a broken planet and a broken financial system. But we are optimists nonetheless. Positive change comes not from blind faith, but through analysis and action. Our aim is to inspire you to be both steely-eyed about the challenges we all face, and excited about how your personal and organizational contribution can matter more than ever. There is much you can do. And there is no end to the fun and fulfilment that can be had in creating great organizations that can enrich people's lives through the quality of the work they offer and the goods and services they craft.

The 80 Minute MBA, then, is not only about the skills and expertise you need to lead and run an organization effectively, but also about the ethics, values and motivations that should be a North Star for anyone seeking to deliver positive change.

We have road-tested our ideas with nearly 100 organizations who have booked us to bring *The 80 Minute MBA* to life for their employees over the last nine years. At those events we are often asked whether we are dismissive of traditional (i.e. much slower) MBAs. We are not. Renowned management theorist Henry Mintzberg has suggested they be scrapped,[2] but we don't agree: the best provide inspiring teachers, opportunities for intellectual interrogation, a challenging peer group and space for reflection.

There is no doubt, however, that the ethos of some MBA programmes has been part of the problem rather than the solution in recent years. The high-octane, risk-taking, money-chasing approach favoured by some MBA graduates may have contributed to the overreach of many firms in the run up to 2008. And the charge sheet against established MBA courses is becoming well known – too narrowly focused on analytical and cognitive skills; an overly stylized and backward-looking treatment of real business problems (the so-called 'case study' method); and at worst, the encouragement of an arrogant, self-centred careerism.[3]

In his book *The Golden Passport*, Duff McDonald does not pull his punches about the role of Harvard Business School: 'Harvard Business School imbues its graduates with the arrogant notion that management is a transferable skill, like driving, and that having pretended to manage for two years, they are now ready to go somewhere and take charge. Worse still, it imbues them with the sense that leadership is something that can be purchased, instead of it being an emergent quality that reveals itself (or doesn't) in the moment in which it is needed.'[4]

Fair criticism? In some cases, yes.

Overblown? Certainly.

A bigger influence on the behaviour of all of us, including MBA graduates and business leaders, is the state of the economy and society. It is no surprise to us that the criticism of MBAs reached its peak at the end of the long boom that ended in 2008. As the trough of rewards got deeper, some leaders resembled greedy animals more than trustworthy stewards of their companies. As recent research confirms, CEOs who begin their careers during booms tend to be less ethical; they adopt riskier financial strategies than CEOs who first entered the workforce in recessions, are more excessively confident in their own abilities, and because they believe they are entitled to better outcomes, pay themselves substantially more than other top executives.[5]

But that was then, and this is now. The fires of recession could help to forge a generation of more ethical, less egotistical leaders. If that sounds like you, keep reading. You are the kind of leader we want to read our book.

Today's challenges require a new spirit of stewardship in business leaders, a new focus on building businesses that are both environmentally and financially sustainable. We focus a good deal of our limited time on sustainability: for this we make no apology. Our planet is broken, and organizations have a responsibility to help fix it. But it is equally important that businesses are economically sustainable too – resting on secure financial foundations, emphasizing organic growth rather than debt-fuelled mergers and acquisitions activity, and rewarding executives for their performance over a period of years rather than months. The broken financial system needs a new approach, a new moral philosophy of business.[6]

There are some things, though, that do not change. One is that no self-respecting business book is complete without a model or diagram. And we're not quite brave enough to do without one. So here's ours,

The 80 Minute MBA 'tornado':

Sustainability

Leadership

Culture

Cash

Conversation

At the very top, as you now probably expect, is **Sustainability**. This book is about success: as a leader, a manager and in organizational terms. But ensuring the future of our fragile, threatened planet must now run through everything we do. The next tornado ring is **Leadership** – a core component of any MBA programme. Then it's the three Cs: culture, cash and conversation. **Culture** – what brings organizations together, why do people matter, how do we engage them? **Cash** – covering finance, balance sheets, accounting, supply chain management and economics. **Conversation** – how do you talk to your markets and your customers? Along the way there are also mini-modules on strategy, ethics, time management, economics, statistics and neuromarketing.

We realize that for some of you even 80 minutes may sound like a big chunk of time to carve out of your hectic schedules. Again, we sympathize: we've had some requests for the '60 Minute MBA', and for the 'half-hour version'. All we can promise is that we'll keep working on it. So, for those of you with no intention of reading any further, our thanks for your time. You've clearly gleaned what you need. If you haven't yet bought the book and the spine is undamaged, you can probably put it carefully back on the shelf (and try to forget that between us we've got five children). If you can spare another seventy-seven minutes, however, we promise not to waste a single one.

SUSTAIN-
ABILITY

We cannot measure national spirit by the Dow Jones Average, nor national achievement by the Gross National Product. For the Gross National Product includes air pollution, and ambulances to clear our highways from carnage . . . The Gross National Product includes the destruction of the redwoods and the death of Lake Superior. It grows with the production of napalm and missiles and nuclear warheads . . . It includes the broadcasting of television programs which glorify violence to sell goods to our children.

Robert F. Kennedy, 18 March 1968

We could keep on as we are: ignoring or playing down the risk and putting responsibility for action elsewhere. But that would mean taking a monumental gamble with our children's future, and a species as intelligent as ours surely wouldn't do *that*. *Would* it?

Mike Berners-Lee and Duncan Clark, *The Burning Question*[1]

When we created *The 80 Minute MBA* a decade ago, not many business schools were focused on sustainability. This was wrong, and we thought MBA curricula should – and would – begin to include environmental considerations. This is one time we are pleased to be proved right: there are now a host of specialist MBAs in Sustainability on the market. The issue is now treated more seriously on almost all MBA courses. Politically, environmental issues have taken a political hit with the election of Donald Trump to the US presidency. But in business, leaders are becoming more environmentally conscious and more aware of the connection between a healthy planet and healthy profits.

We broke the financial system in 2008. but we have been breaking the planet for decades. Some business schools now get it. David Schmittlein, Dean of MIT Sloan, says: 'It's not a story of 28-year-olds trying to save the world. It's a story of managing cataclysmic change. It's about what our students do and need to say when they get into these organizations.'

So who are the change-makers? Environmentally conscious businesspeople are no longer outsiders. Sustainability has been 'mainstreamed' into the corporate agenda over the last ten years.

Eco-activist circa 2007: Lord Stuart Rose, former Chairman and CEO of Marks and Spencer

Eco-activist circa 2016: Tamsin Omond, Head of Global Campaigns at Lush (pictured with Caroline Lucas, Green MP for Brighton Pavilion)

The pioneer on the left is Stuart Rose, former chairman and CEO of Marks and Spencer. Rose does not look like a radical. But his early leadership helped to change the conversation around board-room tables. His 'Plan A' put the retailer in the forefront of the fight against climate change. The five-year, 100-step plan, launched in 2007, committed the firm to becoming carbon neutral by 2012 (a target it successfully met), by reducing the proportion of its waste going into landfill to zero, switching over time to organic cotton, and moving towards fairly traded products.

'We're doing this because it's what you want us to do,' he said at the launch. 'It's also the right thing to do. We're calling it Plan A because we believe it's now the only way to do business. There is no Plan B.'

We don't know what you think of Marks and Spencer. Our own views on the men's fashion lines are, to put it as nicely as possible, mixed. But you didn't buy this book for our views on Blue Harbour. Let us be clear, however: the firm deserves huge credit for its commitment to sustainability. Even as the economic climate puts pressure on the retailer, its commitment to sustainability remains steadfast, with 2017 bringing an updated Plan 2025 and a commitment to become a zero-waste business.[2]

Sustainability in business has come a long way since Rose's decisive but mainstream intervention. The modern face of corporate sustainability activism is more edgy and confrontational – meet Tamsin Omond (shown here campaigning alongside Green MP Caroline Lucas). Omond is Head of Global Campaigns at Lush, the well-known retailer of hand-made cosmetics. (You know, the ones that produce those waves of lavender you walk through in your local shopping centre.) Before joining Lush she was a well-known eco-activist and hard-line campaigner who describes herself as a 'political agitator' on her LinkedIn page.[3]

Lush has taken a strong stance on ethical buying from the outset. As well as a range of targets to reduce their carbon emissions, they also pledge to campaign for environmental issues, empower staff to make a difference, and keep environmental issues at the heart of the business and their decision making. Lush is clearly unusual, but not perhaps as unusual as you think: brand after brand is signalling how seriously it takes this issue.

As part of an 'Every Drop Counts' campaign, Adidas has applied new technology to their fabric dying processes, which now use 100% less water, 50% fewer chemicals and 50% less energy. Unilever has committed to halving the environmental impact of the company's operations and product use by 2030, not only in terms of greenhouse gas emissions but also water consumption, waste and agricultural sourcing. And Google has announced that from 2017 onwards all offices and data centres will use energy provided by purchased solar or wind power (this has required the tech giant to fund enough green energy projects to offset its massive power demands, which in 2015 reached 5.7 terawatt hours).[4]

Successful businesspeople tend to be fact-based sorts of people. And the sheer weight of evidence showing the dangers of climate change in particular is enough to turn any thinking person green.

THE FACTS

'**M**ultiple studies published in peer-reviewed scientific journals show that 97% or more of actively publishing climate scientists agree: Climate-warming trends over the past century are extremely likely due to human activities.'

Who said this? Some bunch of tree huggers?

Here's who: NASA.

Hear that, President Trump? NASA thinks climate change is man-made. You know, the people that send rockets up into . . . Oh, never mind.

Where were we?

Climate change is, of course, the central sustainability issue right now. But the related issues of population growth and resource scarcity fall under the sustainability imperative too. The world's population is forecast to rise from 6.7 billion to 9.2 billion between now and 2050: the increase of 2.5 billion is greater than the total global population in 1950. Most of the usable land in Asia is already under cultivation. That's why the Chinese government is buying land in the Philippines, Uganda, Australia and Mexico. As oil supplies run low, the price of petrochemical fertilizers will rise, making food more expensive: the 2007 price spikes reduced cultivation of Kenya's Rift Valley by a third, according to the BBC.

The 'big one', however, is global warming. The world's climate is being heated by our activities in a way that threatens our own prospects as well as those of other species. We are already losing coral reefs and mountain glaciers, as we have moved closer to a 2° Celsius rise in global temperatures. A rise of 3° Celsius would spell the collapse of the Amazon rain forest, the disappearance of Greenland's ice sheet and the creation of desert across the American Midwest and southern Africa.[5]

Thomas L. Friedman, in his book *Hot, Flat and Crowded*, puts it like this: 'Human society has been like the proverbial frog in the pail on the stove, where the heat gets turned up very slightly every hour, so the frog never thinks to jump out. It just keeps adjusting until it boils to death.' The irony, of course, is that we are turning up the heat on ourselves.

The dwindling, eccentric band of climate change deniers will sometimes point out that levels of carbon dioxide and other gases heating the globe have fluctuated over time. True enough. But you don't have to be a climatologist to look at the following graph – which takes a 400,000-year time frame – and reckon there is something different about recent years. Global average temperature, sea level and Northern Hemisphere snow cover all tell the same story.

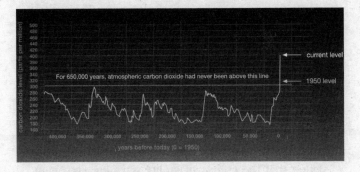

Admittedly, there is huge uncertainty about how quickly the rise in global temperatures will hit weather systems, water levels and crop yields. We just don't know. But the risk is that it will be much worse than we think. The atmosphere is heating up towards a potentially catastrophic 'tipping point'. If you ask experts in the field about their biggest worry, frequently the single word answer is: ice. The reduction of the polar ice is a big worry, because the white caps act as a coolant system, reflecting back the sun's rays.

Melting ice also poses a more immediate threat. First, there is a growing danger that ever larger chunks of ice will slide into the sea, as meltwater loosens the underbelly of the huge ice sheets of Greenland and Antarctica. As we write, Larson C, an ice shelf the size of Bali, has now broken off into the Antarctic Ocean. It is the biggest iceberg ever recorded. Big icebergs mean higher sea levels.

Second, the melting of permafrost in Siberia is releasing dangerous greenhouse gases. The East Siberian Sea is 'bubbling with methane'. There are known to be large stores of the gas underneath the permafrost, which has so far acted as a 'lid' to prevent the gas from escaping. Global warming has put the frozen ground into 'defrost' mode. The tundra is now heating up twice as fast as the rest of the planet. 'Permafrost is a silent ticking time bomb,' says Robert Spencer, an environmental scientist at Florida State University.[6]

Fewer and fewer people now challenge the scientific evidence for man-made climate change. Even in the US, home of climate change scepticism, public opinion is on the move, with 62% of Americans now saying that the effects of global warming are being seen now, 68% that global warming is caused by human activities, and 42% believing that global warming poses a serious threat in their lifetime.[7]

While the charts help, it seems that minds change when the weather changes, in violent and unpredictable ways. In the UK, serious floods are becoming an annual summer event. The impact of Hurricane Sandy on the east coast of the US in 2012 was a tipping point for sections of public opinion in America, with the business bible, *Bloomberg Businessweek*, announcing: 'It's Global Warming, Stupid'.

'You don't claim that an event such as Hurricane Sandy was caused by climate change,' says the Nobel laureate and atmosphere scientist Mario Molina, '[but] the intensity is likely to have increased because of climate change, because of human activities.'[8]

THE BUSINESS IMPACT

Seven in ten UK companies identify a climate change risk with the potential to significantly affect their business or revenue. Half of those (36%) say the identified climate risk or risks will impose a 'high cost' on their operations, according to a survey from The Environment Agency. But businesses see market opportunities too, from climate change adaptation, with respondents identifying one opportunity for every three risks.[9]

These firms are right on both counts. But they need to respond more emphatically to three kinds of business risk caused by climate change:

- PHYSICAL RISKS, INCLUDING RISING SEA LEVELS, EXTREME WEATHER AND CROP FAILURES
- REGULATORY RISKS, E.G. EMISSIONS CURBS AND TOUGHER ENVIRONMENTAL TAX SCHEMES
- REPUTATIONAL RISKS, AS CUSTOMERS, EMPLOYEES AND INVESTORS GO GREEN

PHYSICAL RISKS – DROWNING, NOT WAVING

Who cares about rising sea levels or changing crop patterns? Well, you care if you live on a low-lying island. At the end of 2008, the government of the Maldives embarked on a search for a new home, in readiness to move the entire population when the islands are covered in water: a twenty-first-century Exodus. The Maldives government has now set up a sovereign savings account funded by tourist revenue that will be used to buy land on higher ground.[10]

You should, then, care out of simple human decency. But even in strict business terms, you should also be concerned about the possible impact on your properties, people and supply lines. One obvious example: coastal tourism. Sea level rise will erode and submerge some tourism infrastructure and attractions. Almost a third of Caribbean resorts are less than a metre above the high-water mark. A sea level rise of 1 metre would damage 49–60% of the region's tourist resort properties, lead to the loss or damage of 21 airports and inundate land around 35 ports. The cost of rebuilding tourist resorts in the region by 2050 is estimated at $10 billion to $23.3 billion.[11]

Firms which rely on products that grow in certain threatened areas need to prepare quickly for the likely consequences of global heating. Coffee and chocolate companies whose beans are grown in parts of the world forecast to run out of water; beverage and beer producers who use water in their African and Indian bottling operations. Scarcity is likely to put brands on the defensive. In the past few years, Coca Cola has had to shut down a number of its Indian bottling plants after local farmers blamed the company for using too much water during a time of water scarcity.[12]

REGULATORY RISKS – COUNTING THE (CARBON) COST

Governments have not acted as swiftly as necessary to reduce humanity's climate-wrecking activities. In fact, let's be clear. The early paralysis of some of our national leaders represents the greatest political failure in human history. But recent years have finally given some cause for hope.

In 2016, the Paris Agreement marked a turning point in the battle against climate change. World leaders from across the globe united for the first time in history to legally ratify action against pollution through the United Nations Framework Convention. The landmark international deal saw 194 countries, including the EU and China, sign up to sweeping pledges on the environment at a UN meeting in the French capital in late 2015.

The agreement aims to limit the increase in global average temperatures to 'well below 2° Celsius above pre-industrial levels' – the level beyond which scientists say we will see the worst extremes of global warming. Importantly, it also makes provisions for rich countries to help poorer nations by providing 'climate finance' to adapt to climate change and switch to renewable energy. The pact promises to make an assessment of progress in 2018, with further reviews every five years.

Perhaps you're thinking: Well, I'm glad someone else is looking after this. I plan to work in the software industry (say), and I don't see how I've got any heavy lifting to do here. But the cold reality is that climate change poses a risk to every sector of the economy. Every sector requires energy and has some carbon exposure, including knowledge-based industries such as financial services, pharma or health care. Each company's exposure will depend on business models, strategies, locations, assets and liabilities.[13]

As the collar tightens on carbon emission controls and the cost of carbon rises, clearly some businesses will be more affected than others (coal, oil, gas, natural resource extraction, power generation and utilities, and sectors that are heavy users of energy). But these changes will impact upon all sectors and asset classes. As carbon gets more expensive, business leaders need to adapt, reduce costs, mitigate risks and look for investment upsides and opportunities.

As a consequence, smart investors are looking harder at climate change effects too. A chief executive of a major bank said to one of the authors, 'We need to know how much carbon is in our portfolio.' Not just risk and debt, but how much *carbon*.

Carbon dioxide emissions potential of listed fossil fuel reserves

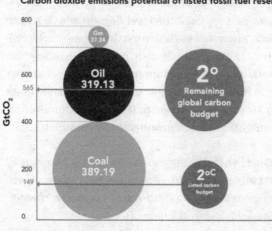

Source: Unburnable Carbon – Are the world's financial markets carrying a carbon bubble?, Carbon Tracker 2011   Carbon Tracker

Successful action to reduce carbon emissions will mean that companies are left with 'stranded assets'. The assets on the balance sheets of major coal and gas companies are 'unburnable' if governments stick to declared carbon budgets, according to Carbon Tracker,[14] [see the graph above], and therefore represent toxic or stranded assets significantly overvalued from a financial point of view. Barclays predicts that Germany's coal generation assets could be effectively worthless by 2030.[15]

Globally, the value of financial assets at risk has been estimated at $4.2 trillion by the *Economist*.[16] For comparison, the annual gross domestic product

(GDP) of Japan, the world's third largest economy, is worth about $4.8 trillion.

CLIMATE CHANGE RISKS FOR BUSINESSES[17]

Liability: *Financial liabilities, including insurance claims and legal damages, arising under the law of contract, tort or negligence because of other climate-related risks*

Transition: *Financial losses arising from disorderly or volatile adjustments to the value of listed and unlisted securities, assets and liabilities in response to other climate-related risks*

Reputational: *Risks affecting businesses engaging in, or connected with, activities that some stakeholders consider to be adding to climate change*

GREEN GOODNESS

If the commercial argument for greener business is good, the moral case is unanswerable. Humankind has broken the planet, but it is not – not quite – too late to fix it. So far our arguments ought to have found favour with the most hard-bitten CFO. If climate change directly threatens the bottom line, either by shattering supply chains or increasing tax bills, the case for business preparedness is clear. But even organizations led by people who understand the seriousness of the challenge find it difficult to make the necessary shift in culture and operations. They are victims of what psychologists call 'path dependency' – in other words, doing what they have always done. But this is now the path to mutual destruction.

Any business that can survive only by threatening the survival of future generations through its polluting activities should not, in fact, survive. The intersection of business and the environment therefore raises profound ethical questions about the purpose and responsibility of business.

system will be an ethical enterprise. And a focus on sustainability is part of a new, properly ethical approach to business.

Business ethics covers matters large and small. According to a survey conducted by MORI for Management Today and the Institute for Business Ethics, 49% of employees said it was 'acceptable' to take pens home from work, while 49% thought it was not. (For the remaining 2% this was presumably too demanding an ethical dilemma.) Of course, given the rise of paperless work, perhaps it's less acceptable to pilfer pens from work – and, oh let's face it, we really don't give a monkey's anyway.

Half the firms surveyed in the UK are providing training in ethics and an increasing number are appointing 'ethics officers'. This is all very well, but the test comes when being 'ethical' conflicts with immediate business goals. Norman Bowie from the University of Minnesota – and author of A Kantian Theory of Leadership – applies the philosophical frameworks of the eighteenth-century philosopher Immanuel Kant to modern debates on ethical leadership. He quotes Kant's kingdom of ends formulation: 'One should act as if one were a member of an ideal kingdom of ends in which one was subject and sovereign at the same time.' Acting as if simultaneously sovereign and subject means that leaders should prepare decisions but not impose them. Here then is Bowie's Kantian leadership test: 'The leader enhances the autonomy of his or her followers.'

The power wielded by a CEO, their capacity to ruin or make lives, means that they have a *disproportionate ethical responsibility. Cooking the books or 'borrowing' from the pension fund to finance high-rolling overseas acquisitions cannot be compared to borrowing a biro.*

For business leaders to win back the trust they have lost, ethics is more than a quick bolt-on or a new-fangled job title. It has to go to the heart of the way they create wealth – and why. 'I have had a few business leaders come to me and ask how they can restore trust,' says Bowie. 'We have had four years of apparently unending scandals, which do seem to have had an impact . . . The days when the MBA was a master of the universe and the CEO was king are over – clearly they have now been knocked firmly off the pedestal.'

Leaders like Ray Anderson, who turned his firm Interface Carpets into an environmental beacon, are contemptuous of those who are unconvinced by the 'business case' for more ethical behaviour. 'I prefer to turn the question round,' he says. 'Where's the business case for double-glazing the planet? Or for destroying the coral reefs?'

In the end, ethics comes down to ethos – which is set by those with the most power in the organization. A reliance on rules and regulations takes us only so far, as the 2008 crisis has demonstrated. 'What I would say is that it should go way beyond compliance,' says Bowie. 'What you need is a leader, a Warren Buffett type, a CEO who embodies an ethics culture.'

There are also dangers in 'professionalizing' ethics. If ethics becomes a matter of following rules, the importance of doing the right thing – acting on 'gut instinct' – could be lost.

Heightened awareness of the climate crisis is rapidly altering the desirability of certain products. It may be that demand for red meat will drop once awareness of its environmental impact grows, for example. Emissions associated with livestock added up to 7.1 gigatonnes (GT) of carbon dioxide equivalent (CO_2e) per year – or 14.5% of all human-caused greenhouse releases, according to the UN Food and Agriculture Organization.[20] It is estimated that a kilo of beef requires between 50,000 and 100,000 litres of water. The average burping, farting cow produces more greenhouse gas than the average four-by-four car.

As well as looking out for ethical customers, smart companies are also becoming alert to the rise of 'ethical employees', who want their employers to be greener. A recent UK study revealed that almost half the workforce (42%) now want to work for an organization that has a positive impact on the world, according research carried out by consultancy Global Tolerance.[21] Employees want to work for companies that match their own values and are doing the right thing. A survey by Adecco found that 52% of employees feel the company they work for should be doing more about the environment.[22]

Climate-wrecking firms might soon become toxic employer brands, in the same way that tobacco companies are today. Campaigners, customers, investors and employees are pressing on the conscience of companies. But in many cases the action is being driven from the boardroom, by a new breed of 'ethical CEOs'. They realize that the search for a cast-iron 'business case' for taking the right action on the environment is often futile, but that the action must be taken in any case. It's not yet clear how far ordinary consumers are voting with their wallets for greener products. Some chief executives now recognize that it is their responsibility to lead consumers, rather than the other way around.

WHAT IS TO BE DONE?

Businesses have a vital leadership role, especially in the face of a politicized environment on climate change. President Trump's now (in)famous tweet about global warming being a hoax dreamed up by the Chinese, and his continued confusion of weather and climate, proved to be the precursor for his decision for the US to exit the Paris Climate Change Agreement.

What matters here are the facts and the risks. The facts on warming, and the risks of failing to reach demanding targets on decarbonization to hold the global temperature increase to less than 2° Celsius by 2050. You can tell how far the corporate debate has come when Citigroup publicly denounced the president's decision on the Paris accord and committed to finance $100 billion in clean energy, infrastructure and technology projects.

Business leaders need to:

• ASSESS THEIR EXPOSURE TO RISKS – PHYSICAL, REGULATORY AND REPUTATIONAL – FROM CLIMATE CHANGE

HSBC has calculated that fossil fuel equities could fall by 40–60% in a low emission scenario[23]

• MOVE TO FULL DISCLOSURE OF ENVIRONMENT IMPACTS, INCLUDING CARBON EMISSIONS

In 2015 France became the first country to introduce mandatory carbon reporting by investors, by introducing Article 173 of the Energy Transition for Green Growth Bill, which requires institutional investors to disclose how they manage climate risks.[24]

- SUPPORT AND COMMIT TO DEMANDING INTERNAL TARGETS FOR CARBON REDUCTIONS

Businesses and cities need to step up if national governments step back, and align their environmental goals with climate science. So, for example, business should join the We Mean Business coalition (https://www.wemeanbusinesscoalition.org), alongside existing members such as Mars, Renault, Ikeda, Sony and Astra Zeneca, and adopt the science-based targets it supports. It calls for companies to commit to a set of targets to control climate change, including:

a. EP100 — Companies commit, over 25 years, to doubling their economic output from each unit of energy (energy productivity)
b. RE100 — Companies commit to using 100% renewable electricity
c. Zero deforestation — Companies commit, by 2020, to using no commodities that cause deforestation.

As We Mean Business puts it: 'You'll get return on your investment. You'll cut costs. You'll become more competitive. You'll see your reputation flourish.'[25] So . . . what are you waiting for?

- LOBBY GOVERNMENTS FOR TOUGHER REGULATION TO ENSURE A LEVEL, GREEN PLAYING FIELD

Business leaders should not fight regulation, but the opposite. They ought to proactively argue *for* regulatory frameworks that help them scale clean energy and energy efficiency, conserve national resources and send the right price signals to drive investment in low carbon technologies.[26]

- LOSE THE PREOCCUPATION WITH ENERGY SOLUTIONS — AND ADOPT AND SUPPORT A WIDER RESPONSE

Renewable energy sources are an obvious — and vital — element in a decarbonization movement. But there are less obvious solutions too, as recent research ranking interventions by their potential carbon impact has shown.[27]

The number one solution, in terms of potential impact? A combination of educating girls and family planning. Together these could reduce 120 GT of CO2e by 2050 — more than on — and off-shore wind power combined (99 GT). Both reduced food waste and plant-rich diets (on their own) beat solar farms and rooftop solar combined. Sitting at the very top of the list, with an impact that dwarfs any single energy source: refrigerant management. So we don't have to wait for a Hail Mary technological innovation to make much faster progress.

(If you were wondering what you can do personally, here are three simple steps: throw away less food, eat less meat, and get a new fridge with the best possible energy efficiency rating.)

From GreenTech to new sharing economy business models and platforms, companies have the potential to unleash a wave of innovation in low carbon technologies and practices. The result will be new products, services and employment – oh, and saving the planet. It should not be a surprise that tech companies like Apple, Amazon, Google and Microsoft are leading the green charge.[28]

New forms of collaboration are emerging, too. Retailers compete in terms of price and service, and we want them to. But there is no reason they shouldn't work *together* in some areas, such as logistics. What's the point of one retailer having a half-empty lorry coming over from France, while a competitor does exactly the same? Why not share the lorry? Why not share the warehouse? Why not share the distribution networks? Similarly, firms can act in concert to improve supplier standards across the board, for example on greener packaging. Companies can bring down their carbon emissions by smart collaboration in the non-competitive elements of their business. This environmentally driven collaboration with competitors is called *co-opetition*, an essential skill for the executive of the future.

Every MBA course is about success of one sort or another. Most people undertaking an MBA – or reading this book – want to become more successful in terms of their own career: to earn more, acquire more power, have more impact. Great. We have absolutely no problem with these ambitions. We share them. *The 80 Minute MBA* contains advice on achieving success as a leader, a manager and a boss; success in creating workplaces full of energy and productivity; success in enriching your conversations with your customers and, of course, success in building piles of cash. But the challenges of climate change require us to reconfigure our notions of success; to not only think about more robust, fairer forms of business and markets, but also to begin the patient, painful task of healing the planet.

If success in any of those other domains comes at the cost of our children and grandchildren, then it is no kind of success worth having.

Even the hardest-hearted are realizing that green is the new black.

LEADER-
SHIP

> [Leaders are] individuals who help
> us overcome our own selfishness,
> weakness, and fears, and get us to
> do harder, better, more important
> work than we could do on our own.
>
> David Foster Wallace, *Consider the Lobster*[1]

Here's the bad news: five books on leadership are published on a typical day.[2] This torrent of advice on leadership is enough to provoke an anxiety attack in the staunchest executive. Now for some good news: the majority are so bad that they can be safely ignored. Bad books on leadership fall into one of two main categories. First, a famous business leader puts their photo on the front and writes a book with a single, dispiriting message: 'If Only You Were Me You'd Be As Famous And Successful As Me'. Second, a connection is made between leadership and a religion, organization or fictional character. What can we learn about leadership from 'Moses CEO', the toys you loved as a child or US Navy SEALs? Answer: nothing.

Now for some properly bad news. In what will be seen as the halcyon years before 2008, the lamentable quality of most leadership advice didn't matter quite so much. But now, as we collectively struggle to reboot the economy and move towards a cycle of improving productivity and growth, the need for real reflection on what business leadership means is urgent. The necessary remoralization of the market will place new ethical and personal demands on leaders. The cult of the CEO, overpaid and over-confident, has come to a shattering end. Business leaders now look like Shelley's Ozymandias, 'king of kings'. Their glittering city of a debt-fuelled, finance-driven capitalism has been razed – and leadership will never look quite the same again. Neither the ancient Greeks nor early Christians would have been surprised by the events of 2008. The Athenians believed that insufficient humility before the gods – what they called *hubris* – would result in destructive forces being unleashed: the *nemesis*. This was a message reinforced in the Old Testament: 'Pride goes before destruction, and a haughty spirit before a fall' (Proverbs 16:18). Another verse of Proverbs explains why this is so: 'Every one who is arrogant is an abomination to the Lord; be assured, he will not go unpunished.'

Against this backdrop, the question 'Why should anyone be led by you?' acquires new force. It is the question asked by Rob Goffee and Gareth Jones, professors at the London Business School, in an influential article and book of that title. It is absolutely the right one. Anybody who aspires to lead must understand that the power of leaders stems, ultimately, from their followers. The motivation of the follower – the 'why' in the question – is critical. Power can be imposed upon people, but successful organizations need leaders who draw power out of others whilst equipping everyone that follows them to succeed.

BOOKS TO IGNORE

Given the deluge of leadership advice, we want to help to guide your further reading by giving some areas to avoid. As a general rule, ignore books that put an adjective in front of the word 'leadership'. This will put plenty of books on your non-reading list – there is something of an adjectival arms race in this section of the market. Always keep in mind that a statement only has some value if a person can reasonably maintain the opposite. Leadership, it is variously argued, needs to be of the following kind:

- LIVING – RATHER THAN DEAD LEADERSHIP OR CORPSING LEADERSHIP, WHICH WE'VE ALL EXPERIENCED AT SOME POINT IN OUR CAREER
- COURAGEOUS – DEFINITELY BETTER THAN COWARDLY!
- SPIRITUAL – RATHER THAN, SAY, RADICAL ATHEIST LEADERSHIP
- RESONANT – AS OPPOSED TO DISSONANT. FACED WITH THE CHOICE BETWEEN THE TWO, WHO DOESN'T WANT TO RESONATE?
- PRIMAL – RATHER THAN, SAY, SECONDARY. (ACTUALLY THIS ONE IS PERHAPS THE EXCEPTION TO THE AVOID ADJECTIVES RULE, SINCE IT'S ACTUALLY RATHER GOOD, IN SPITE OF THE TITLE)
- SERVANT – BRITISH PM TONY BLAIR DECLARED IN 1997, 'WE ARE THE SERVANTS NOW.' YEAH, RIGHT
- LIQUID – OF COURSE HUMANS ARE MOSTLY WATER, WHICH HELPS. BUT YOU MUST AVOID BEING TOO SOLID. AND GASEOUS LEADERSHIP IS WORST OF ALL

THREE THINGS TO FORGET

Leadership books and theories can be daunting. Readers are often left with the impression that they need to be good at everything, to be a super-person who is intellectually strong, emotionally literate, decisive yet understanding, charismatic and down-to-earth, visionary and realistic. So we want to give you a whole bunch of things to stop worrying about and spend less time on: charisma, your weaknesses and strategy.

Some brief explanation is probably in order.

CHARISMA

You can forget about charisma for two reasons. First, there's no evidence that charismatic leaders are more successful – if anything, the opposite may be true. Second, charisma cannot be taught or learned. If you're not charismatic, you are never going to be. So forget about it.

YOUR WEAKNESSES

You're a natural self-improver; you're reading this book after all. But self-improvement brings pitfalls, the most dangerous of which is the idea that you should work hard on your weaknesses. As far as the authors are concerned, that would be a paralyzing full-time job. And when it comes to your leadership performance, over-focusing on your weaknesses is a very bad idea, as long as, of course, your weaknesses are not having toxic impacts on others.[3]

One of the more welcome insights of the past 15 years is that strengths-based leadership works. Exceptional leaders often have *skewed profiles*, displaying extraordinary prowess in one or two areas of expertise or ways of thinking, while being absolutely terrible at everything else. They focus on their strengths and delegate tasks they're less good at to others who are more skilled or experienced.

One of the things you can be sure of is that you are rubbish at certain things (we're sorry to break that to you if it's news), and you will *always* be rubbish at certain things. You are unbalanced. If you spend all your time trying to get better at the things at which you're intrinsically rubbish, you won't get on with the job of being a leader. Great leaders are necessarily unbalanced; they just *know* they are.

STRATEGY

Last but not least, don't worry about strategy. We are aware that this is a slightly controversial statement: most MBA courses spend months teaching strategy skills. So we'll spend a tiny bit longer on this one (see the display box below). But if you're already half-convinced, here's the short version: it's not making strategy that counts, it's putting it into practice. As Elvis wisely put it, 'A little less conversation, a little more action'.

STRATEGY

There's a dirty truth about strategy. It's nearly always over-resourced inside organizations. Why? Because too many businesses have a silver bullet delusion about strategy – gripped by the notion that if we just get our strategy perfect we'll differentiate ourselves and beat the competition. Unfortunately, strategy is nowhere near as important as some organizations and leaders think it is.

Of course it matters.

In their excellent book Hard Facts, Dangerous Half-Truths and Total Nonsense: Profiting from

---

Evidence-based Management, *Jeffrey Pfeffer and Robert Sutton encourage you to imagine a business as a collection of iron filings on a piece of paper. A good strategy lines them up, establishing common purpose and directing resources behind a clear set of goals. It tells organizations what to focus on and, almost as importantly, what not to do. But organizations should stop chasing the perfect strategy. The key differentiator for business, what makes the difference between successful and less successful, is the ability to execute. Richard Kovacevich, reflecting on his successful tenure as CEO at Norwest, had this to say about the relative importance of strategy and execution:* 'I could leave our strategic plan on a plane and it wouldn't make any difference. No one could execute it. Our success has nothing to do with planning. It has to do with execution.'[4]

Clearly good leaders think hard about getting the interaction between strategy, implementation and execution right. It is hard to implement a poor strategy well and doubly difficult to produce excellent results with a poor strategy that's being poorly implemented. Equally, a great business strategy does not guarantee success; you've still got to implement and execute well.[5]

As Larry Bossidy and Ram Charan argue in their book Execution: The Discipline of Getting Things Done, *leaders are spending too much time strategizing, philosophizing and pontificating.* 'People think of execution as the tactical side of the business,' *they write,* 'something leaders delegate while they focus on the perceived "bigger issues". This idea is completely wrong.' *Bear in* mind that execution is the major task of a business leader and this becomes a pretty damning statement.

The ability to do both things well – strategy development and strategy execution – is a rare skill in senior leaders. Only 8% of leaders are good at both strategy and execution, and 35% of leaders are neutral or worse at both.[6]

So why is strategy such a resistant creature inside businesses?

Let's reveal the terrible secret about strategy. For leaders and MBA students, strategy is the activity where they can still feel powerful in a world where they increasingly don't feel powerful. Strategy-making has therefore become the required caffeine hit for an active executive team. It suits business leaders to talk endlessly about 'disruption' and 'revolution', about game-changing new technologies which demand a new response. Yet the evidence of the past ten years, as the impact of digital has played out across business, is that successful businesses don't choose between using digital technologies as a way to improve existing operations or using digital as a platform for new growth. Rather they do both, optimizing the current business model and building resilience while creating next generation business models. They strategize and execute in dynamic equal measure.[7]

Overall, the message for leaders is clear: make things happen. As Adam Crozier, who has just completed a stellar term as CEO of ITV, said to his staff: 'Top CEOs will all say what makes a great leader are those people who make things

HEROES

One of our greatest business heroes is an unassuming man called Darwin E. Smith. Darwin was the Chief Executive of Kimberly-Clark from 1971 to 1991. When he took over, KC was a struggling paper company. Here is the firm's performance BD (Before Darwin):

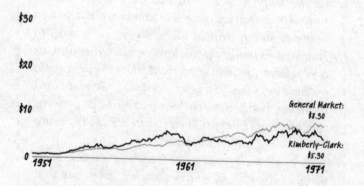

Before Darwin Smith
Kimberly-Clark,
Cumulative Value of $1 invested, 1951–1971

In the years BD, Kimberly-Clark was, if anything, actually slightly underperforming in the general market. Now look at the years AD:

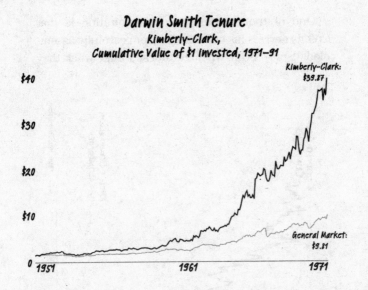

Darwin Smith Tenure
Kimberly-Clark,
Cumulative Value of $1 invested, 1971–91

Kimberly-Clark:
$39.87

$40

$30

$20

$10

General Market:
$3.81

0

1951   1961   1971

During Darwin's tenure, KC outperformed the general market by a ratio of something like four to one and became one of the most successful companies in the world. Darwin was asked in a rare press interview to describe his leadership style. He paused, blinked behind his thick glasses and finally said, 'Eccentric'. Those of you who know your management literature will recognize elements of this story, which is told brilliantly by Jim Collins in his book *Good to Great – Why Some Companies Make the Leap and Others Don't*. Our views on leadership have been strongly influenced by Collins (and his sometime collaborator Jerry Porras). Actually, 'influenced' is a bit mealy-mouthed; we have slavishly followed their lead. But here's the thing: we think Collins's research is sound and his conclusions robust. His findings are also borne out by our own experience of working with leaders and leadership teams. We love Collins.

One of the reasons for our admiration is that Collins derives his conclusions from carefully assembled data – even when he doesn't find what they

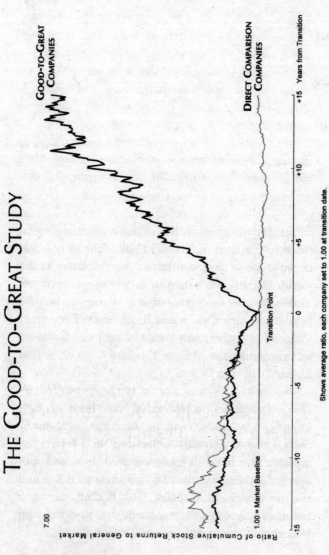

THE GOOD-TO-GREAT STUDY

GOOD-TO-GREAT COMPANIES

DIRECT COMPARISON COMPANIES

Transition Point

1.00 = Market Baseline

Ratio of Cumulative Stock Returns to General Market

7.00

-15   -10   -5   0   +5   +10   +15   Years from Transition

Shows average ratio, each company set to 1.00 at transition date.

were looking for. In *Good to Great*, Collins was looking to see what made some companies exhibit a step-change in performance. The graph opposite shows the trajectory of the 11 he identified.

Collins was not looking for leadership attributes to explain the change in direction. In fact, because lazy researchers often retreat to a mantra of 'it must be the leadership' to explain differences in performance, Collins told his team not to focus on the boss. But the data was unequivocal. The quality of the CEO turned out to be a critical factor in explaining why a company became great: the 11 companies identified outperformed the market, on average, by a factor of seven in the 15 years after an obvious 'transition point' in performance.

Smith thought himself eccentric, but in fact his approach bore a strong resemblance to that of the other ten leaders: George Cain, Alan Wurtzel, David Maxwell, Colman Mockler, Jim Herring, Lyle Everingham, Joe Cullman, Fred Allen, Cork Walgreen and Carl Reichardt. Don't worry if you haven't heard of them either; it reveals not your ignorance, but their wisdom. In retirement, Smith explained, 'I never stopped trying to become qualified for the job.'

THE LEADERSHIP WIKI: FOUR THINGS GREAT LEADERS KNOW

Being a successful leader is less about who you are or what you do than about what you know. The term 'wiki' stands for 'what I know is' and a successful leader's internal wiki includes four key pieces of knowledge: *where* the organization is heading; *what* is going on; *who* they are; and *how* to build a strong team.

WHERE WE'RE GOING

The first thing successful leaders know is where the organization is going. This sounds obvious, but that's not always the case. Plenty of nominal leaders subscribe to the approach satirized by the nineteenth-century French radical Alexandre Ledru-Rollin as: 'There go my people. I must find out where they're going, so that I can lead them.'

Take our hero Darwin E. Smith. When he took over Kimberly-Clark, he realized that the future of the firm lay not in paper, but in paper products like tissues, diapers and paper towels. That's where the margin was. This meant that the firm no longer needed to own its own paper mill, so he said that they would sell it. Not an easy call, given the location of the mill: Kimberly. That's a big, bold decision. But Smith made it very clear from the outset: *that's* where we're going; we're getting out of *this* market and into *that* market – and he never deviated from that view. Everyone knew where the organization was going. A key ingredient in the culture of a successful organization is that everyone knows its destination – its animating purpose – and, crucially, the contribution of their own efforts. (This is a theme we pick up in the section on Culture.)

Charles R. 'Cork' Walgreen, who ran the family firm Walgreen's from 1971 to 1998, made a similar decision to take the firm out of food-service operations and focus on pharmacies. His successor, Dan Jorndt, recalled how, after months of discussion, Cork announced at a board meeting: 'OK, now I am going to draw a line in the sand. We are going to be out of the restaurant business completely in five years.' According to Jorndt, 'You could have heard a pin drop.' Not surprising, given that at the time the firm had over 500 restaurants. But the direction was crystal clear, and Jorndt reported that Cork 'never doubted; never second-guessed'. At a planning meeting six months later, a manager repeated the aim of shedding the restaurants within five years. Cork said: 'Listen, you have four a half years. I said you had five years six months ago. Now you've got four and half years.' This incident had a galvanizing effect: the whole organization quickly understood that he actually meant five years. One of the most commonly reported failings of leaders is, paradoxically, an unwillingness to use their authority. This is not a problem with the leaders whose organizations are most successful. They are not bullying or hectoring, but they are authoritative. Authority without arrogance: that's the secret.

WHAT'S GOING ON?

Successful leaders build, in Collins's phrase, a 'culture of discipline'. They are about getting things done, managing information effectively in order to inform decisions, control costs and marshal resources. If this sounds a little unglamorous for the titans of the corporate world, this is because of the unfortunate division made in recent years between leadership and its slightly grubby cousin, management. The business analyst Warren Bennis wrote: 'Management is about doing things right; leadership is about doing the right things.' It was a much repeated sentence, and an unhelpful one.

The trouble with the leadership–management dichotomy is that it lets bosses off the hook when it comes to constructing good management information systems and scrutinizing the results – tracking the development of projects, peering into departmental accounts and generally keeping their arms around the organization. Once leaders start talking about 'keeping their eyes on the horizon' or taking a 'helicopter view', sell your shares and/or start looking for a new job. As the business writers Bruce Pasternak and James O'Toole correctly lament: 'We now know many companies have been overled and undermanaged.' Leaders were so busy being 'strategic' that half the time they didn't know what the heck was going on in their own organizations.

There is no better example of the danger of this leadership–management separation than the financial crash of 2008. Tom McKillop, chairman of the Royal Bank of Scotland in the years prior to the crisis, admitted before the Treasury Select Committee in February 2009 that he did not understand the details of the financial instruments he had to approve. A profound failure of leadership.[8]

In contrast, the 11 successful leaders from *Good to Great* were the sort who were happier spending their evening with the monthly management accounts than at a swanky New York dinner. You *do* have to sweat the small stuff. Great leaders also keep in touch with how people are feeling. Successful leaders do not spend their whole time worrying if everyone is happy. But they do know what the emotional temperature of the organization is.

The excellent work by Daniel Goleman and his colleagues on emotional intelligence, or EQ (which includes *Primal Leadership*), shows that good leaders are emotionally in tune with the people in their organization. Knowledgeable leaders understand that people are not machines to be reprogrammed according to the latest strategy document. In particular, they understand that change provokes an emotional response, and that successful change involves allowing people some space to feel angry, resentful and afraid as well as excited, hopeful and energized.

In her insightful book *The Change Monster*, Jeanie Daniel Duck describes the emotional roller-coaster that characterizes profound organizational change, and how a failure to allow for the emotional aspects of change scuppers the entire enterprise. As Duck writes, 'Emotions are data. In any transformation, there are common patterns that can be identified and accurately analyzed with real rigor and rationality. With understanding, there are a variety of ways to address potential problems successfully.' But it is important not to confuse EQ with a need for constant soul-searching. Leaders need to be open and emotionally sentient. But nobody is going to follow a self-scrutinizing wimp. What great leaders achieve is the right balance of inward-looking and outward-looking behaviour.

FOCUSED AND ATTENTIVE?

'A primary task of leadership is to direct attention. To do so leaders must learn to focus their own attention.'[9]

Daniel Goleman suggests that leaders need to cultivate awareness and focus in three distinct ways: focusing on yourself, focusing on others and focusing on the wider world.

They need to be attentive to how they are balancing their time and efforts across this 'triad of awareness'. Focusing inward and focusing constructively on others helps a leader cultivate the primary elements of emotional intelligence. A fuller understanding of how they focus on the wider world can improve their ability to devise strategy, innovate and manage organizations.

Ask yourself – do you have that awareness in abundance and in proper balance? If you've never asked yourself, do so quickly, for as Goleman notes: 'A failure to focus inward leaves you rudderless, a failure to focus on others renders you clueless, and a failure to focus outward may leave you blindsided.'

WHO AM I?

Successful leaders know who they are. They know where they're strong. But they know their weaknesses too. There's a fierce humility to successful leaders. They know they can't do x, y and z. They do not presume that they are all-conquering. They are willing to hire people as talented or more talented than themselves to fill senior positions around them.

A realistic assessment of personal performance provides a vital clue to leadership potential. In an important article, 'What We Know About Leadership', psychologists Robert Hogan, Gordon Curphy and Joyce Hogan summarized a substantial body of research comparing the assessments by leaders of their own performance with the views of their colleagues.[10] The leaders whose self-appraisal matched the judgement of those working for them were the ones who were most likely to succeed, while those who overrated themselves were far and away the worst leaders.

The successful leaders of the *Good to Great* companies were, says Collins, 'a study in duality: modest and wilful, humble and fearless'. The individuals were fairly humble about themselves but not about their organizations: they combined 'personal humility with intense professional will'. Most importantly, they cared about the success of their organizations rather than their own personal success. It's not about getting on the front cover of *Fortune* magazine or being active on the speaker circuit. For them, it is not about being a great business leader, but about leading a great business. More than 1,000 years ago, the author of *Beowulf*, the epic Anglo-Saxon tale, wrote: 'Behaviour that's admired is the path to power among people everywhere.' It is important, then, for us all to admire the right kinds of behaviour in our leaders. Particularly when humility hits it out of the park.

HUMILITY AND LEADERSHIP

'The research is clear: when we choose humble, unassuming people as our leaders, the world around us becomes a better place' —Margarita Mayo.[11]

At first glance, this seems quite a claim for humble leaders. But the research evidence is strong and growing. A recent study of 105 small-

Those who become successful leaders tend to be socially skilled too, able to pick up on social cues in their interactions and 'judge the mood' accurately. Leaders who fail – and at least half suffer from what US researchers graphically dub 'executive derailment' – are generally not lacking technical skill, ambition or intelligence. It's their character that lets them down. As Hogan and colleagues write: 'Many managers who are bright, hard-working, ambitious, and technically competent fail (or are in danger of failing) because they are perceived as arrogant, vindictive, untrustworthy, selfish, emotional, compulsive, overcontrolling, insensitive, abrasive, aloof, too ambitious, or unable to delegate or make decisions.' And that's on a good day.

You might be thinking that surely not many managers could display those characteristics at work. But a recent Interact/Harris Poll of US workers uncovered a series of symptoms of poor emotional intelligence, ranging from micromanaging to bullying, narcissism and indecisiveness. Half said their company executives refuse to talk to subordinates.[14]

This represents a quiet daily crisis in our workplaces.

HOW TO BUILD A STRONG TEAM

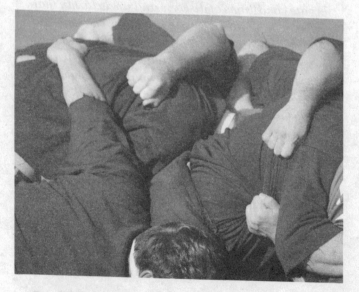

Successful leaders are motivated by what they *build* rather than what they *get*. Most importantly, great leaders build great teams. They surround themselves with talented people – people with talents that they do not possess themselves and know they do not. As President Harry S. Truman reminded us, 'You can accomplish anything in life, provided you do not mind who gets the credit.'

This is one of the reasons why their companies continue to succeed long after they've gone. Very often, strong leaders build the team first, then decide where to go. With the right people, you can go to different, better places. We have said that great leaders have a clear sense of direction, of where the organization is going. But very often this is the result of collective decision-making in a talented team.

Because the future holds so much uncertainty, a team with the agility to retask, seize new opportunities and question received wisdom is more important than a single dominant vision. 'The old adage "People are your most important asset" is wrong,' says Collins. 'People are not your most important asset. The *right* people are.'

So how do you build great teams? Focus on three things:

1. MAKE HIRING YOUR HIGHEST PRIORITY

'What is the single most important thing you do at work? Hiring . . . The most important skill any business person can develop is interviewing . . . and the simple truth is most people are not good at it.' So say Eric Schmidt and Jonathan Rosenberg.[15]

If it isn't already, make hiring the most important activity that your leaders and managers take part in, and build a shared vision of your organization's hiring *Do's and Don'ts* (see Google's helpful prompts in the display box below). If you can only have one hiring rule, make it this one:

- **DON'T COMPROMISE IN HIRING PEOPLE. HOLD OUT FOR THE BEST RATHER THAN SIMPLY PLUGGING THE GAP**

GOOGLE'S HIRING DO'S AND DON'TS

Google hiring panels live by the following rules:

- *Hire people who are smarter and more knowledgeable than you are*

- *Don't hire people you can't learn from or be challenged by*

- *Hire people who will add value to the product and the culture*

- *Hire people who inspire and work well with others*

- *Don't hire people who prefer to work alone*

- *Don't hire people with narrow skill sets or interests*

- *Hire people who get things done*

- *Hire people who are ethical and who communicate openly*

- *The urgency of filling a role isn't sufficiently important to compromise quality in hiring*

- *Hire only when you've found a great candidate*

- *Don't settle for anything less*

2. KEEP TEAMS SMALL AND GIVE THEM A CLEAR, COMPELLING PURPOSE

We've worked with many 'teams' in organizations which were too big and loosely bound together to be anything of the kind. You may have heard of Amazon CEO Jeff Bezos's famous 'two-pizza team rule', that teams shouldn't be larger than what two pizzas can feed (i.e. four or five people). For Bezos, small teams stay focused, communicate better, move faster and secure high levels of autonomy and innovation.[16]

Teams also need a clear common purpose: a compelling reason to shape their efforts, and related challenging goals to keep them focused.[17]

3. DIAL UP COGNITIVE DIVERSITY

Teams made up of members who have different perspectives and different styles of processing knowledge achieve better results. These key features of cognitive diversity are not predicted simply by gender, ethnicity or age, but also social and professional background and modes of thinking. The key message is try to avoid setting up like-minded teams, and recruit team members for their cognitive diversity. As Alison Reynolds and David Lewis, researchers on team diversity and effectiveness, put it: 'There is much talk of authentic leadership, i.e. being yourself. Perhaps it is even more important that leaders focus on enabling others to be themselves.'[18]

HURRY SICKNESS

Successful leadership takes time. Time to know yourself and colleagues. Time to make good hiring and firing decisions. But time may feel like the scarcest resource of all. You may be suffering from what James Gleick, in his book Faster: The Acceleration of Just About Everything, *calls hurry sickness. Here's a Hurry Sickness Test, adapted from Gleick – a quick one, of course, which you can administer to yourself.*

- *When you brush your teeth in the morning, are you always doing something else at the same time – finding underwear, choosing a shirt, yelling at the kids?*

- *When you just catch a train or a plane – jumping on a moment before the doors close – do you secretly get a kick out of it? Is it worth missing the odd one to get that rush, to enjoy the feeling of having wasted a nanosecond with all the losers in the departure lounge?*

- *When you get into a lift, do you immediately look for the 'door-close' button? You're not alone. 'It gets more used than any other button in the elevator,' says John Kendall, Director of Advanced Technology at Otis Elevator Company. 'When they're in the elevator they want to go.' This is despite the fact that the delay – technically known as 'door dwell' (see, it's just dwelling) – is between two and four seconds. Four seconds? It's unimaginable you'd wait that long, isn't it?*

- *When you call a lift and it all looks good – the button makes a 'bing' noise, the light comes on and stays on – do you, if it does not arrive within a certain period of time, go back and press the button again? Thought so. One of our clients said, 'No, I don't go back and press it again: I HOLD IT DOWN.' Now, if you think this action will in fact speed the arrival of the lift, we can't help you. Although at least you are behaving rationally. The rest of you are doing something you know to be irrational. Why? Because it's killing you. Those 10, 15, 20 seconds are killing you.*

Count how many questions you answered yes to.

Scores:

0 = So laid-back, you are virtually horizontal. Time to get a job?

1 = Buddhist levels of hurry health.

2 = Not too bad at all; you control time well.

3 = Early symptoms of hurry sickness.

4 = Chasing your own tail most of the day, advanced stages of the disease.

5 = Whoa! Slow down, tiger! (Or buy a portable defibrillator.)

We are acutely aware that discussing the dangers of hurry sickness in the context of The 80 Minute MBA *is ironic or paradoxical or – yes, all right – downright hypocritical. Guilty as charged. We should indeed heal ourselves. But we can all surely agree about the danger of confusing business with busyness; of packing our diaries with meetings in order to avoid any real work; of lacking the time to reflect on organizational direction; of feeling unable to have proper conversations with colleagues. Ideally, you should schedule a day out of the office each week, or keep half the day free of meetings (or do a digital detox as you stay offline for a few hours to think and reflect). Few of us live in such an ideal world, but you can at least make a start in the important goal of changing your relationship with time. Just leave the lift button alone.*

One way to test the 'teaminess' of a leader is their attitude towards succession. Great leaders want great successors and usually find them within their own ranks rather than in the 'global marketplace' for CEOs. But a selfless attitude to succession does not come easily to all. Management expert Manfred Kets de Vries writes: 'I've often said, tongue in cheek, that the major task of a CEO is to find his most likely successor and kill the bastard.' Less successful leaders are those who take a certain delight in the way the company crashes after they leave. They can then say, 'Well, it was all about me then, wasn't it? Look what happened as soon as I left.' *Après moi le déluge*. What better evidence for your own brilliance than the crashing and burning of the next in line? 'It is not enough to succeed', Gore Vidal reminds us. 'Others must also fail.'

In this sense, Jack Welch – who we bet you *have* heard of – is an antihero of business leadership. It is undeniable that General Electric performed strongly when he was at the helm, not least because of his intense focus on cost-cutting and throwing out the weakest-performing staff (although it is worth pointing out that the *Good to Great* companies did much better). In an interview with the *Financial Times* in July 2008, Welch said, 'You can look at it any way you want and I don't care what you say. We had 425,000 employees and $25bn of business. When I left we had 310,000 and $125bn, five times the revenue, 25 per cent fewer people.' The comment reveals Welch's considerable belief in his own abilities. His talk is not about the skills of the team around him, or of needing to continue to learn anything himself. When GE missed some important targets following his departure, Welch went on TV to warn that he would 'shoot' Jeff Immelt, his successor, if he did not rectify the 'screw-up'. (Welch retracted the following day, but it was an insight into his mindset.)

The finest leaders are those with bigger ambitions for their organization than for themselves. They know that the greatest strength of an organization lies with its people, and in its *culture* – the focus of our next chapter.

CULTURE

While the world's workplace is going through extraordinary change, the practice of management has been frozen in time for more than 30 years. According to Gallup's World Poll, many people in the world hate their job and especially their boss.[1]

Far and away the best prize that life offers is the chance to work hard at work worth doing.

Theodore Roosevelt, 1903 Labor Day Address

Only 15% of employees around the world say they feel engaged at work, according to the latest 2017 Gallup world poll. And we wonder why productivity has been sliding for decades. That miserable engagement figure is only up 2% since 2013. This leads us to conclude, perhaps a little selfishly, that nowhere near enough people have read this chapter of *The 80 Minute MBA*, on the central importance of culture.

We are in the midst of an employee engagement emergency. The necessary treatment is to change our workplace cultures and how people are managed and encouraged to give of their best. If you're in HR, here's the good news: your moment has arrived.

Unfortunately, we've never been very fond of the phrase *human resources*. It conjures up dusty images of administration-obsessed personnel functions. The 'human remains' jibes have definitely damaged the brand. *Culture* is a better way of framing the challenge of people and organizations – encouraging a necessary focus on how to make our workplace cultures fit for purpose and fulfilling for employees and enterprises alike.

It is a self-evident truth that organizations need to care about their culture. People are simultaneously the most valuable factor of production and the most difficult to engage effectively. Not many organizations operate as if they have accepted either of these inconvenient truths.

PEOPLE = VALUE^x

Let's start with the most familiar workplace cliché: 'People are our greatest asset.' The two questions that should be posed in response are:

Do leaders mean it?

Is it true?

To which the answers are:

No – or at least not enough.

Yes. It is true.

In our experience, most senior executives – despite their public protestations to the contrary – are not fully convinced that the ultimate success of their firm depends on how well they manage, engage and invest in their people. To be fair, this is partly because it has proved difficult to establish clear, irrefutable evidence that investments in the workforce boost business performance.

Nearly all CFOs recognize the critical impact of

human capital in key business areas such as driving customer satisfaction, product/service innovation, growth and overall profitability, according to a CFO Research Services report. But only 16% said they truly understood the return on their human capital investments.[2]

As a result, the process of engaging employees is often too time-consuming and the performance payback too slow for an impatient CEO. But it is quite clear that labour, or what economists call *human capital*, has a unique ability to create value in the modern economy. As we've moved from an industrial to a knowledge economy, 'hard' physical assets, such as buildings and machinery, have become less important (though of course still vital in many sectors). *Intangible assets* – non-monetary assets that cannot be seen, touched or physically measured, such as intellectual property, innovation and knowledge – are the motors of value inside modern enterprises. They now account for up to 80% of the value of large companies.[3]

In 1984, the 'book value' of the top 150 US public companies – in other words, what their physical assets could be sold for on the open market – made up about 75% of their stock market value, according to a paper by US private sector economists Robert J. Shapiro and Nam D. Pham. By 2005, the book value of the top 150 companies had dropped to just 36% of their market value. The remaining two-thirds of value lay in their intangible assets, in particular intellectual property (IP).[4] In straight economic terms, people contribute more value to businesses than any other factor of production. Knowledge workers now make up 60% of the UK workforce and are the single fastest growing segment.[5]

Investment patterns have followed suit. Recent UK evidence suggests that business investment in intangible assets continues to outstrip investment in tangibles. In 2011 the UK market sector invested £137.5 billion in knowledge assets, compared to £89.8 billion in tangible assets.[6]

ALGORITHMICALLY YOURS?: NEW ERA EMPLOYEE ENGAGEMENT

The much heralded 'rise of the robots' (see display box below) isn't going to diminish the value-adding power of human capital. It will in fact enhance it, as your staff and freelancers learn to work alongside and with smart machines. Most artificial intelligence experts agree that in the future, organizations will be staffed by some combination of smart robots, smart thinking machines and humans, with humans doing those tasks that complement technology or that technology can't do well.[7]

You might think you're going to be devoting a lot less of your leadership time to creating the right workplace culture. Who needs to nurture a machine, after all? If you don't think of yourself as a 'people' person you might already be getting excited about the predictions that, in a host of areas from productivity to wellness, algorithms are going to be vital tools in creating new era employee engagement. In human resources, algorithms are already transforming talent acquisition as they are able to rapidly evaluate the suitability of candidates for specific roles. And the same technology could easily be applied within an organization to allocate workloads to the right people.[8]

Employees, as consumers, are already familiar with behaviour influencing through contextualization algorithms introduced by e-commerce companies such as Amazon to profitably influence billions of shopping decisions (of which more in the Conversation section). But don't relax just yet. It's more complicated than that, as you might expect.

RISE OF THE ROBOTS

The prediction that automation and artificial intelligence will profoundly reshape the labour market and workplace is old; like, mid-life old, cited by President Kennedy in 1963.[9] But in recent years a strong consensus has emerged that the impact is going to be big and is going to happen more quickly than we previously predicted. A widely cited paper by Frey and Osborne of Oxford University, exploring the 'automatability' of work, predicted that 47% of jobs in the US are at risk of computerization in the next two decades.[10]

More recent work by the Organisation for Economic Co-operation and Development (OECD) focused instead on the potential for automation of tasks within jobs, rather than of occupational categories as a whole. The conclusion was that while many workers will see their jobs change as certain tasks are automated away, only about 9% of jobs are fully automatable.[11]

Let's split the difference. Big change is coming, and fast. In the near term (the next 15 years) automation is clearly going to replace a significant proportion of tasks and jobs but will not replace people or employment. Human capital will be freed up to focus on important and value-creating tasks.[12] *As Kevin Kelly notes: 'The AI on the horizon looks like Amazon Web Services – cheap, reliable, industrial-grade digital smartness running behind everything, and almost invisible except when it blinks off. This new utilitarian AI will also augment us individually as people (deepening our memory, speeding our recognition) and collectively as a species.'*[13]

The real challenge for all of us, leader and led, is whether we are ready to make the most of the opportunities this presents for our economy and society: as Andrew McAfee says, 'The Industrial Revolution was about overcoming the limitations of our individual muscles. What is going on right now in the second machine age is overcoming the limitations of our individual minds.'[14]

Time to hardwire for humanity, given that the 'business plans of the next 10,000 startups are easy to forecast. Take X and add AI'.[15]

Most employees will become familiar with technologies and algorithms that seek to positively influence our behaviour at work. Companies are already experimenting with persuasive tools and algorithms which build in 'nudge' and 'reward triggers' into employee's everyday task and activities – sometimes called the 'gamification' of work. For example:

- JPMorgan Chase has introduced an algorithm to forecast and positively influence the behaviour of thousands of employees to minimize mistaken or ethically wrong decisions.

- Richard Branson's Virgin Atlantic teamed up with economists in an experiment that used influence algorithms to guide its pilots in using less fuel, resulting in savings of 6,828 metric tons of fuel worth £3.3 million.
- Cisco UK uses an algorithm-based people management app that obtains insight into how its employees view the world, leveraging that

knowledge to energize its 72,000 employees and to persuade managers to adapt their approach to reorganization.[16]

Gartner are already recommending to their clients that they should be looking to 'exploit persuasive algorithms that address the perpetual business need of talent retention and attraction. Build trust and transparency to avoid "algorithm aversion" and allay fears of infringing on workers' rights. Algorithms must benefit both the organization and the worker – not one or the other.' The understatement around 'algorithm aversion' is a pearl.

If this all sounds a bit like Corporate Big Brother, a potentially dystopian world of real-time data monitoring and manipulation, we hear you. We confidently predict that it won't be long before we see the first batch of legal cases with claimants filing discrimination claims against algorithms that go wrong in the workplace. If it's not yet on your HR 'to do' list, checking AI tools and algorithms for racial, gender, age and other common biases soon will be.[17]

Cathy O'Neil, in her brilliant book *Weapons of Math Destruction*, warns how easy it is for algorithms made with the best of intentions to 'encode human prejudice, misunderstanding and bias into their software systems'.[18] Happily for all of us (unless, horrible thought, you're a machine reader of this book), non-human intelligence is 'not a bug' in the workplace, 'it's a feature'.[19] And a feature that will get more valuable by the hour.

Which means that however AI and automation play out, the challenge of new era employee engagement looks a lot like old-era employee engagement, namely creating workplace cultures that are high on values and principle, low on control, and full of purpose-driven emotional engagement.

As Ed Hess, Business Professor at the University of Virginia Darden School, writes: 'Machines will take over many aspects of the operational excellence inside organisations. So, we have to ask ourselves: In order to innovate, what's going to be the differentiator? The answer, I say, is the quality of the human component of the business – how good your people are at thinking and emotionally engaging with their teammates . . .Technology will require businesses to become much more *humanistic people-centric* places built on psychological principles, not just economic or strategic principles.'[20]

So how do we create people-centric cultures that will thrive in the future?

COMMITMENT SEEKERS

The stakes have been raised on the people front. The mini-industries that have grown up around the so-called 'war for talent' and offering *employee engagement* solutions reflect companies' desire to get more from their people. What makes human capital special – its humanity – also makes it harder to coordinate and inspire. You don't hear managers complaining about lazy steel rods. The holy grail for organizations – and the factor which often separates successful organizations from the rest – is getting people voluntarily to give more of their best. It's what we call the *commitment dividend*.

The commitment dividend comes from employees who care about the organization's aims, who willingly make improvements, contribute ideas and take decisions – all symptoms of high levels of discretionary commitment. Managers talk about employees who are prepared to work 'beyond contract' – in other words, their commitment to the job extends beyond the narrow confines of their job description. But this is not just about motivating individuals. Successful teams and organizations are greater than the sum of their parts. The strength of the relationships and networks – the *social capital* – in the firm is a key determinant of productivity.

It is, by now, hopefully even more blindingly clear that people matter. The economics of human capital in the coming AI era make this truth stark. And the point is not simply that the work of people is intrinsically more valuable, but also that the harder they work and the better they work together – commitment dividend plus social capital – the more successful the organization will be.

So what do we do about that? How do we motivate people? How do we engage employees? Money, perks and physical environment count for relatively little. Or rather, getting them wrong is seriously demotivating, but getting them right is not what lights a fire inside people. They are what the influential management theorist Frederick Herzberg calls 'maintenance' or 'hygiene' factors. What actually releases the commitment dividend – the factors Herzberg calls 'motivational factors' – has more to do with quality of relationships, levels of individual discretion and the prevailing organizational ethos. As Herzberg puts it: 'If you want someone to do a good job, give them a good job to do.' There is a considerable literature on reward systems and performance-related pay. We would not recommend spending too much time in this particular thicket. The goal should not be a high-tech reward system, but rewarding work.

FORMING CULTURES

First, though, a quick word on the way organizational cultures are created, sustained and altered. All MBAs will contain a 'culture change' module. But this language is not quite right. Organizational cultures, rather like mould, grow. Of course, they grow in new directions, sometimes as a result of deliberate executive intent, more often as a consequence of historical accident and fate.

And organizational cultures are highly resistant to 'culture change' programmes, consultants and projects. It is not big-change programmes that change culture, but the accumulation of thousands of small actions – what are sometimes known as *micro behaviours* – over time. Behaviours are the threads of any social fabric. The philosopher Gerry Cohen, writing on social justice in his marvellously titled book *If You're an Egalitarian, How Come You're So Rich?*, puts it like this: 'I now believe that a change in social ethos, a change in the attitudes people sustain towards each other in the thick of daily life, is necessary for producing equality.' We love that phrase 'in the thick of daily life'. Because it is in the thick of everyday working life that cultures are created – or destroyed.

There are plenty of firms which declare themselves in favour of flexible working and work–life balance, but all the manager has to do is glance at his watch as you leave, or make a 'joke' about being a part-timer when you come in late, or roll their eyes when you say you'd like to work from home. There are plenty of firms that stress their commitment to gender equality, but in which staff stick sexist screen-saver images on their computers, or suggest someone has only been hired 'because of her t***' (which proved to be an expensive piece of prejudice).[21] There are plenty of organizations that proudly declare their green credentials, but then fly the entire senior management to the Mediterranean for an annual strategy session, aka knees-up.

And the more senior and powerful an individual is, the greater the impact of their own behaviour – for good and for ill. Apologies for the obviousness of this statement. But we have been struck by the number of senior executives who claim that a particular course of action is not possible because 'the culture round here won't allow it'. To which the response has to be: but it's *your* culture. As a senior manager or executive, you have a huge impact on the culture simply through the way you conduct yourself each day. For example, a number of work-place studies have shown the sizeable impact of a boss saying 'thank you'. The more senior a position a person holds, the more power they have to shape the culture and climate of their organization. This is a power which too few leaders take seriously enough.

What kind of culture, then, should managers try to help create? A successful organizational culture has three key features: solidarity, energy and autonomy.

SOLIDARITY

Solidarity sounds like a powerful Polish trade union from the 1980s. And of course it is, one which under the leadership of Lech Wałęsa – who went on to become president of Poland – played a significant role in bringing about the end of the Communist regime in that nation and helped to spark the 1989 revolutions across Eastern Europe. But if it seems like an odd word, we think it's the right one. Solidarity captures two related factors: *community* and *purpose*. Solidarity means that 'we're all in this together'.

A community is built upon sociability. Small surprise, then, that the most consistently powerful predictor of job satisfaction, productivity, and loyalty is the answer to the following question: 'Do you have a close friend at work?'[22] Having a pal at work is vital to a sense of sociability. This finding should be put alongside the evidence that people most often cite their relationship with their immediate superior as a reason for quitting.[23] 'Toxic bosses' remain one of US employees' biggest problems at work, with 41% of American workers saying they've been 'psychologically harassed' on the job.[24]

The importance of relationships is clear: people stay for their mates and leave because of their managers.

Sociable workplaces are those where gossiping by the water cooler is not seen as a semi-criminal activity; where investments are made in physical spaces for people to interact; and in which the Christmas party is never, ever cancelled.

Communities are built on relationships, which in turn are built on *conversations*. Most organizations are now over-communicating with themselves – not least because of the ease of e-mail – but under-conversing. As Theodore Zeldin argues in *Conversation* (a brilliant book), conversations can go 'off-agenda', lead anywhere, mix up diverse topics and are conducted without hierarchy. They are the synapses of the organizational brain – spaces in which sparks are ignited. (They are also the way smart firms conduct their relationships with other vital stakeholders, including customers, as we'll argue later.) But, of course, organizations are not just running a kind of social club, a place to sit with a cappuccino, flirt and talk about the weekend. There's stuff to do, a common purpose to be pursued. That's what solidarity means: a community with a purpose.

In the previous section we discussed the importance of leaders being able to establish a clear sense of purpose and direction: to know and communicate where the organization is going. People need to know what the organization is trying to achieve, but also how what they're doing on a day-to-day basis contributes to that goal. You have probably heard the story of the NASA cleaner, who when asked by a visiting bigwig – perhaps even a president (JFK or LBJ) – 'What do you do?' answers, 'I help to put men on the Moon.' This story may well be apocryphal – at any rate, we cannot source it satisfactorily. The fact that there is a similar story about a stonemason, Christopher Wren and St Paul's Cathedral makes us even more sceptical. But the tale continues to be told because it is a perfect example of a worker seeing a clear connection between their day job and the organization's overall purpose. There is a clear *line of sight* between daily, individual exertion and long-term, collective goals. It enables employees to feel motivated and accountable for what they do, and at best to demand the same of others.

Goffee and Jones give the example of the insurance company New York Life, a mutual founded in 1845, which has distilled the essence of this bond for its employees: 'You know who you are and how your actions affect others . . . you question those whose actions appear inconsistent with our values.'[25] But what very often happens is that at some point in the organization that line of sight is lost, so that people feel as if they're shovelling bits of paper around, adding up columns of numbers or cleaning toilets, none of which appears to connect with the purpose of the organization. They lose, with desperate results, the sense of ownership that a clear line of sight brings.

ENERGY

For many years the most evocative description of a company culture was the phrase coined by the London Business School's late, great Professor Sumantra Ghoshal: 'the smell of the place'. We've always struggled a bit with this. The smell of a place can depend on the state of the air-conditioning or the volume of perfume on a receptionist. It seems to us that 'energy' is a better way of capturing the essence of an organization's soul. Never mind the smell: feel the vibe.

We're not huge Jack Welch fans, to be honest. We much prefer Darwin E. Smith. But Welch does capture, in his '4 Es of Leadership', some of the most important ways in which leaders shape their organizations' culture. The first two Es are 'positive energy' – working with enthusiasm and enjoyment – and 'the ability to energize others . . . to get other people revved up'. (The other two Es are 'edge', or 'the courage to make tough yes-or-no decisions', and 'execute – the ability to get the job done'.) Welch is absolutely right. A CEO of a major publishing company we've worked with said to us, 'I've come to the conclusion that my job is simply injecting energy into the right part of the organization at the right time.'

DRAINS AND RADIATORS

In life, there are people who are *drains* and those who are *radiators*. If you go out for a drink for an hour with a drain, you'll need another drink afterwards to recover. They've drained your energy out of you. Your battery level's flatlined. But spend an hour with a radiator and you'll end up with a bit more of a spring in your step yourself. They've energized you. (Hopefully you haven't drained it all out of them.) But institutional practices can also act as drains or radiators. A useful exercise is simply to ask people what these are in your organization.

Does the 'motivational' session raise energy levels? Or is it something else? What depletes energy? Meetings are a commonly cited example. This is why meetings always have biscuits and coffee in them. The mere fact of being in a meeting is draining the energy out of the participants so quickly that they have to shove it back in – in the form of sugar and caffeine – simply in order to survive for the next hour. If meetings are the problem, have fewer of them, have fewer people in them, and make them more effective.[26] Find out where the radiators and drains are located in your organization and see whether or not it's possible to improve levels of energy. And guard your own energy levels: if you're running on empty, you can't energize others.

Schmidt and Rosenberg again: 'Meetings are not like government agencies – they should be easy to kill.'[27]

AUTONOMY

Last, but certainly not least, is autonomy: giving people more freedom. The more freedom people have over where, how and when they work, the happier and more productive they are. We have highlighted the importance of the commitment dividend or discretionary effort, and it is important to recognize that greater discretionary effort goes hand in hand with enhanced workplace freedoms.

There are a number of dimensions in which autonomy really counts: in terms of how the job is done, what the job consists of and where the work is done. There are, needless to say, serious restrictions in how far some staff can be given flexibility – and, indeed, in how much they want. But as a general principle, far greater autonomy over both task and time could be granted to the majority of employees.

NETFLIX'S GROWN-UP CULTURE

Netflix has rightly been gaining attention for its pioneering HR practices. They motivate people through purpose and performance, not process and policies. We like their no-nonsense, autonomous approach to working time, and particularly to paid leave.

Their old policy for paid leave was:

- *10 vacation days*

- *10 holidays*

- *Sick days*

Their new guidelines for paid leave:

- *Take whatever time is appropriate*

- *Work it out with your boss and colleagues*

So no caps, and work it out for yourself.

The policy wasn't entirely without rules. If you wanted 30 days off in a row, you needed to meet with HR. And senior leaders were urged to take vacations and to let people know about them—so they were visible role models for the policy.

Put simply, Netflix sought to give its employees more freedom by removing the paid leave caps, and trusted them to do the right thing. Which they do. Because their culture is strong and they hired the right people in the first place.[28]

Let's talk about employee influence over what work and tasks get prioritized, and what employees should focus on. A good litmus of a workplace full of energy and autonomy is whether it's intelligently democratized. Do your employees feel able to challenge senior staff about key processes, priorities and decisions? Learn from Google here, and make sure your HIPPOs aren't abolishing autonomy (see display box below).

DON'T LISTEN TO THE HIPPOS

Google has a highly democratized and autonomous culture. You may know some of the headlines already, including Google employees being encouraged to spend 20% of their time working on whatever they choose.

An even more noteworthy inoculation against an over-controlled culture, is their attempts to neutralize the dangerous influence of Hippos – the Highest Paid Person's Opinion.

Described in detail by Eric Schmidt and Jonathan Rosenberg in their enlightening book How Google Works *(see above, 'Leadership', note 15), the company works hard to create a workplace where it is the quality of the idea that matters, not the seniority of the person who suggests it.*

Ahead of the weekly company-wide meeting, in which senior executives run a no-holds-barred Q&A session, questions and ideas get submitted blind (no listed author) and are then circulated to each employee so they can vote for their favourite. Those questions and ideas winning the most votes are the ones that get discussed at the meeting. And of course those questions are never exclusively from the most senior people.

No Analytics? Welcome to the HIPPO*

@timoelliott

*Highest Paid Person's Opinion

What about another litmus test of autonomy, working hours? Are you working in an organization actively creating a working culture that encourages and rewards effort and excellence and not presence? Rather than the slightly depressing phrase 'work–life balance' (which is based on three flawed assumptions: life is good, work is bad, and they're divisible), or the technocratic term 'flexible working', we advocate *time sovereignty*. The key is that individuals have the maximum degree of control over their time, allied to the motivation to give of their best in every aspect of their life. Your job as a leader is to create a culture which gives them some choices about how they deliver their best to your company. As Schmidt notes: 'The best cultures invite and enable people to be overworked in a good way, with too many interesting things to do both at work and at home . . . Manage this by giving people responsibility and freedom. Don't order them to stay late and work or to go home early and spend time with their families. Instead, tell them to own the things for which they are responsible, and they will do what it takes to get them done. Give them the space and freedom to make it happen.'

Amen. Are you working in a workplace like that? If not, maybe it's time to find a new one. Or change the one you're in.

Does your employment contract state a specific number of hours you should work? Do you know what the number is? If so, do you work them? Quite.

We all know that an arbitrary number of hours 'worked' – and especially 'worked' in the office – is a terrible measure of somebody's effectiveness. But there are still some organizations that manage people like that. It's a bit like managing a nursery class. 'Knell?' 'Yes, Miss.' (Tick present.) 'Reeves?' 'Yes, Miss.' (Tick present.)

Technology means that physical presence is increasingly becoming an outmoded proxy for productivity. The vast majority of workers today don't have a fixed desk or computer, with company work-spaces averaging an occupancy rate of only 39%,[29] and we all know that technology allows us to work when we're not at work – with smartphones, tablets and wi-fi-enabled laptops keeping us constantly in touch and able to work all the time and anytime. (This means, of course, that time sovereignty really does have to mean sovereignty: you must use the awesome power of the off button on those occasions when you want to stop working.)

But it is important to consider the other side of

the coin: technology also allows us *not* to work when we *are* 'at work'. There's a wonderful chapter in *Dilbert: The Joy of Work*, by Scott Adams, headed 'Reverse Telecommuting'. The office has now become the ideal place to keep in touch with your friends, buy a lamp on eBay, update your insurance policy or find a holiday – but, thanks to our friend the computer, it looks exactly like work.

If you are the boss, or the wrong side of 35, or lack digital dexterity, perhaps you doubt the ubiquity of these practices. Ladies and gentlemen of the Liberated Workforce Jury, it is time for Exhibit A. When a mainstream online computer magazine – take a bow *PC World*, from IDG – is giving tips to its readers on how to 'stealthily slack-off at work whilst appearing to be working', you might finally realize that your eyes have been deceiving you as you have contentedly watched your intent 'working bees' in your open-plan office.[30]

This 'slacking-off' in plain sight has even been monetized. Where there's laziness there's lucre. Fancy playing a game that looks like a spreadsheet? The slacking expert at *PC World* brought a gift – a slacking site new to us (a surprise, as we thought we knew all of them) deliciously called Can't You See I'm Busy (http://cantyouseeimbusy.com) which fulsomely delivers on their brand promise, namely: 'All the games at CantYouSeeImBusy.com are designed in a way that nobody can see that you're gaming. In fact, your boss and colleagues will think that you're working harder than ever before.'

And just in case you are now feeling outraged and think *PC World* is irresponsibly undermining the productivity pillars of workplaces across the land, they do end with a helpful bonus tip: 'Get some actual work done too. We don't blame you for wanting to unwind a little at the office, but your boss very well might. So don't just slack off perpetually. Strike a balance, be productive, and use these tips with discretion.'

Dear Reader, please use all slacking tips responsibly. Remember, you're an MBA student, headed for greatness.

The point is not – repeat, not – that you should start clamping down on this sort of thing, introduce spy software or institute rules about how many minutes each day employees are 'permitted' to use the internet for 'personal use'. For one thing, it won't work. For another, it's dumb.

If an employee fails to deliver, your performance-management systems will pick it up and you can fire them on the perfectly reasonable grounds that they are not doing their job.

If your performance-management system will not, in fact, pick up the fact that someone is not doing their job, we humbly submit that it is your performance-management system you really need to look at, or your new 'nudge and reward' algorithm, not your policies on working hours or personal internet use.

SET YOUR PEOPLE FREE

If you set people free and simply trust them to do their job, we offer two guarantees. First, some people will abuse your trust. They will use their time sovereignty to avoid work altogether, or to do as little as humanly possible to prevent getting fired. Second, it will be worth it anyway. Those who abuse a freer system are the same people who are abusing your current system by turning up on the dot of nine, leaving on the dot of five and doing nothing other than the bare minimum in the meantime.

Time sovereignty does require a high degree of trust – and it is not only bosses who are sceptical. Fellow employees often think that their co-workers will do less at home, and if the balance of home and in-office time isn't right for these workers, colleagues can report difficulties in collaborating with them. It's easier to communicate, solve problems and have casual collisions with co-workers in person.[31] So the disease of presenteeism is not confined to the management classes, but it is managers and leaders who need to cure themselves of it most urgently.

You may have a nagging feeling that solidarity and autonomy rest uneasily together. If everyone is self-governing, free-wheeling around and working from home, how can they be part of a united team? We confess to the same anxiety. There is a tension here. But the rise in home-working is being driven by people who work from home for a day or two a week rather than all of the time.

The need and desire to be in the office, with colleagues, are unalterable facts of organizational life. Skype, Slack and e-mail are powerful tools. They are necessary – but not sufficient. They cannot support the building of communities of purpose or the generation of organizational energy. But it's equally clear that great teams do not need to be together all of the time: world-class sports teams might train together two or three days a week at most. It is obviously a good idea to have some times of the week when the team tries to be together – rather like the market days of old.

Beyond this, set your people free.

If you succeed in creating a solidaristic, energetic

and autonomous culture, you will ensure higher levels of job satisfaction among your staff or team – and therefore a happier, more trusting and engaged workforce. But this is not your only measure of success. This kind of culture will also promote innovation, extra effort and higher productivity. Cold, hard cash: the subject of our next section.

When I asked my accountant if anything
could get me out of this mess I am in
now he thought for a long time and said,
'Yes, death would help.'

Robert Morley

If God only gave me a clear sign;
like making a large deposit in
my name at a Swiss bank.

Woody Allen

Financial literacy is as important as
reading and writing. It's an essential
skill for full participation in society.

Alison Pask, London Institute of Banking and Finance[1]

JUST WHAT IS ACCOUNTING ANYWAY?

It's often asserted that accounting is the language of business.[2] The conduct of business is certainly unimaginable without it. At its broadest, accounting has been defined by the American Accounting Association as 'the process of identifying, measuring, and communicating economic information to permit informed judgements and decisions by users of the information.'

There – that's got you interested. It's a good job accountants don't run the sales and marketing department. An equally accurate definition of accounting might be: 'You will never consistently make money, control your costs, make the best use of your resources, or be able to decide where to focus your efforts inside your business unless you understand the fundamental rules of accounting.'

If you're going to run any enterprise, you have to understand the language of accounts. Fortunately, you can make sense of accounts with a comparatively limited vocabulary. To set you on your way, we have provided a glossary of financial terms at the end of this chapter.

AN ANCIENT ART

The power and relevance of accounting are underscored by the longevity of its central tenets – some of the basic rules of accounting haven't changed since ancient Rome. Let us introduce you to the real Godfather.

Luca Pacioli (1445–1517) was a Franciscan friar who produced the first printed description of the double entry accounting system in 1494, in order to 'give the trader without delay information as to his assets and liabilities'.[3] We hope Luca would smile on our efforts to summarize the key foundations of accounting.

THE FOUR GOLDEN RULES

Accounting is fundamentally a rule-based discipline. A fully fledged MBA accounting model would equip you with a plethora of rules, on both the practice of accounting and on widely accepted public standards of reporting financial information. Our ambition here is much more limited: to provide you with the four key tenets of financial accounting that will give you the necessary financial literacy to understand a set of basic accounts.

What are they?

- A DOUBLE ENTRY SYSTEM INVOLVES RECORDING THE EFFECTS OF EACH TRANSACTION AS DEBITS AND CREDITS
- LEFT-HAND SIDE OF AN ACCOUNT IS THE DEBIT SIDE, AND THE RIGHT-HAND SIDE IS THE CREDIT SIDE
- TOTAL DEBITS MUST EQUAL TOTAL CREDITS
- THE ACCOUNTING EQUATION: ASSETS = LIABILITIES + CAPITAL

The problem, of course, is remembering these rules – until now, that is.

GOLDEN RULE 1: A DOUBLE ENTRY SYSTEM INVOLVES RECORDING THE EFFECTS OF EACH TRANSACTION AS DEBITS AND CREDITS

The cornerstone of the double entry system is that

each transaction is recorded with at least one debit and one credit.

This is because each party in a business transaction will receive something and give something in return. In book-keeping terms, what is received is a debit (something comes 'IN' when looking at the entry of a debit item) and what is given is a credit (something is going 'OUT' when looking at the entry of a credit item). This should alert you to the vital fact that the words *credit* and *debit* have a very specific meaning in accounting, different from their use in everyday language.

So, for example, let's say that *The 80 Minute MBA* company pays cash to buy a photocopier for £500. How would this transaction be recorded as a debit and a credit? As the table below shows, if we think of a debit as something coming 'IN' there would be a debit entry in the Machinery account, and if we think of a credit as something going 'OUT' there would be a credit entry in the Cash account.

EFFECT	BOOK-KEEPING ACTION
Photocopier comes IN	A _debit_ entry in the Machinery account
Cash goes OUT	A _credit_ entry in the Cash account

GOLDEN RULE 2: THE LEFT-HAND SIDE OF AN ACCOUNT IS THE DEBIT SIDE, AND THE RIGHT-HAND SIDE IS THE CREDIT SIDE

If every transaction creates a debit and a credit, how do we record them in our accounts? Which is where Golden Rule 2 comes in – namely that the left-hand side of an account is always the debit side and the right-hand side of the account is always the credit side.

In its simplest form, an account consists of three parts:

- **THE TITLE OF THE ACCOUNT (ITS NAME)**
- **A LEFT OR DEBIT SIDE**
- **A RIGHT OR CREDIT SIDE**

Because the alignment of these parts of an account resembles the letter T, it is referred to as a T account.

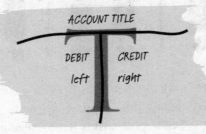

You will also sometimes see T accounts depicted to represent a scale or balance. If this feels like a new or unfamiliar rule, think of your bank statements – your current account statements – which adopt the same convention of debits on the left and credits on the right.

And the overall accounts of a business are, in simple terms, the amalgam of a wide range of different T accounts which feature in any business, such as assets, liabilities and capital.

Part of the *hard yards* in accounting is remembering how different types of transactions are recorded in different T accounts. Again, clear rules apply and are summarized in the diagram below, which features in any standard accounting textbook. All asset accounts are increased with debits and decreased with credits. Liabilities and capital work in the opposite way to assets.

Rules for Double Entry

Before we leave Golden Rule 2 we want to make sure you're getting this. Think debits and credits – now shut your eyes. Were you seeing them automatically on the left and right – debits left, credits right? If not, we have a simple suggestion to help you remember.

Look at the letters below.

AC / DC

When we think of AC/DC we think of Angus Young, Gibson SG guitars and the best rock and roll band ever. If you didn't, perhaps you thought power supply instead. Either way – although we prefer the rock reference – think whichever you choose, but think AC/DC. Look at the order of the words.

Think every account (AC) comprises of debits and credits (DC).

Think DC: debits come before credits.

Think DC: the D is on the left, the C is on the right. Debits on the left, credits on the right.

Think debits and credits – shut your eyes and try again.

$$AC \, / \, DC$$

Account (entries) must be / Debits (left) and Credits (right)

GOLDEN RULE 3: TOTAL DEBITS MUST EQUAL TOTAL CREDITS

If you can remember our earlier diagram of a T account shown as a balance scale, you should never forget Golden Rule 3: that after every transaction is recorded in the company accounts, total debits must equal total credits.

Back to our recently purchased *The 80 Minute MBA* photocopier – which was paid for in cash, at a cost of £500 – our book-keeping entry would read:

ACCOUNT	DEBIT	CREDIT
Machinery	£500	£0
Cash	£0	£500

In this example, the books stay in balance because the exact pounds sterling amount that increase the value of our Machinery account decreases the value of our Cash account.

GOLDEN RULE 4: THE ACCOUNTING EQUATION

Thus far we have seen that every transaction must be recorded once on the debit side of an account and once on the credit side of an account, and that total debits must equal total credits.

In this way, double entry bookkeeping follows the strictures of our final golden rule – the accounting equation[4] – which states that

$$\textbf{Assets = liabilities + capital}$$

It is a mathematical equation and the equals sign (=) requires that both sides of the equation stay in balance at all times. In other words, the equation must be in balance after every recorded transaction in the system. What does the accounting equation mean in simple terms? Namely that the economic resources of a business (the assets) must be equal to the claims on those economic resources (liabilities + capital). What you have should be equal to what you owe.

Assets consist of property of all kinds, such as buildings, machinery and stocks of goods. Other assets include debts owed by customers and the amount of money in the bank account. Liabilities include amounts owed by the business for goods and services supplied to the business and for expenses incurred by the business that have not yet been paid for. They also include funds borrowed by the business. Capital is often called the owner's equity. It comprises the funds invested in the business by the owner plus any profits retained for use in the business less any share of the profits paid out of the business to the owner.[5]

So back to the idea of an entity as made up of resources and claims on those resources. A good way to think of the accounting equation is captured in the diagram below.

Business misery results when the claims on an entity's resources continually outstrip its resources.

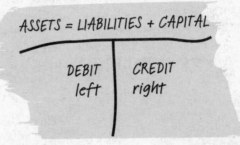

ASSETS = LIABILITIES + CAPITAL

DEBIT   CREDIT
left   right

The Accounting Equation

FROM EQUATIONS TO T ACCOUNTS TO BALANCE SHEETS

Whilst you may not have heard about the accounting equation before, you will undoubtedly have heard about a balance sheet before, which is simply the accounting equation expressed in a financial statement.

The balance sheet documents the accounting equation at a particular point in time. As the name implies, and as determined by the accounting equation, *it has to balance* – i.e. the value of the assets must be equal to the claims made against those assets.

When one looks at a balance sheet, you can see our four golden rules threaded through it, with debits on the left, credits on the right and the need for balance.

The link between the accounting equation and normal T accounts is a simple one. Debits are positive numbers that are represented on the left side of the accounting equation, and credits are positive numbers represented on the right side of the accounting equation.

ASSETS		LIABILITIES	
Cash at bank	£1,000	Accounts payable	£1,000
Accounts receivable	£1,000		
Photocopier	£500	Total liabilities:	£1,000
		CAPITAL	
		John Knell	£750
		Richard Reeves	£750
		Total capital:	£1,500
Total:	£2,500		
		Total:	£2,500

The same financial and spatial relationships are replicated in the presentation of a balance sheet, as our example below shows. Happily, *The 80 Minute MBA* is as yet a simple business.

'THE 80 MINUTE MBA' BALANCE SHEET AT THE END OF PERIOD 1

ASSETS		LIABILITIES	
Cash at bank	£1,000	Accounts payable	£1,000
Accounts receivable	£1,000		
Photocopier	£500	Total liabilities:	£1,000

Who said understanding accounts was complicated? Just remember our four golden rules. Or, more simply, remember:

AC/DC

And remember that what you have should be equal to what you owe. For those about to balance, we salute you.

FINANCIAL ACCOUNTING GLOSSARY

Asset: an asset is something a company *owns* which has future economic value (land, buildings, equipment, goodwill etc.).

Liability: a liability is something a company *owes* (money, service, product etc.).

Revenues: amounts received or to be received from customers for sales of products or services (sales, rent or interest).

Capital: often called the owner's equity. It comprises the funds invested in the business by the owner and what's left of the assets after liabilities have been deducted. Profit: revenue less costs.

The profit and loss account: summarizes a business's trading transactions – income, sales and expenditure – and the resulting profit or loss for a given period.

A balance sheet: provides a financial snapshot at a given point in time listing all of the assets and liabilities of a company.

A balance sheet shows:
- Fixed assets – long-term possessions
- Current assets – short-term possessions
- Current liabilities – what the business owes and must repay in the short term
- Long-term liabilities – including owner's or shareholders' capital

The balance sheet is so called because there is a debit entry and credit entry for everything, which must balance.

The balance sheet shows:

- How solvent the business is
- How liquid its assets are – how much is in the form of cash or can easily be converted into cash, i.e. stocks and shares.]
- How the business is financed
- How much capital is being used

These definitions are drawn in large part from www.businesslink.gov.uk and supplemented by some material from Woods, F. and S. Robinson (2004) *Book-Keeping and Accounting*, FT Prentice Hall.

INSTANT ECONOMICS

People who have studied economics tend to be quite a self-satisfied bunch. Fair enough: it's a difficult, technical subject. They look upon those unacquainted with the core concepts of the dismal science with a mixture of pity and contempt. Given the limits on your time, a three-year degree in economics followed by a doctorate in econometric modelling is probably not on the cards. But the killer line which economists often use is, 'Well, can you at least draw supply and demand curves?' Any MBA worth their salt must be able to meet this challenge and dash off the basic supply and demand model on the back of a napkin, or on a newspaper in the back of a cab.

DEMAND

Demand is an expression of how much people want something, measured in terms of how much they're willing to pay for it – or, to put it slightly differently, how much of it they'll buy at a certain price. So here's how a demand curve for, say, widgets might look.

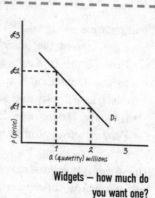

Widgets – how much do you want one?

You may notice that the 'curve' is, in fact, a straight line. This is a trick to try to catch out non-economists – always call it a curve. Price (P) is measured on the vertical axis and quantity (Q) on the horizontal one. (We remember the order by thinking of the phrase 'Mind your Ps and Qs', but we're pretty sure we are alone in this.) D1 is the demand line – yes, very good, the curve – and represents a given level of demand for the widgets in question. At this level of demand (D1), consumers will buy 2 million widgets for £1, or 1 million for £2. Demand is rarely static, however, and of course the goal of the widget supplier's marketing department is to raise the level of demand so that people will pay more for the widgets or buy more at the same price. If widgets become all the rage, the demand curve will shift upwards. At this higher level of demand (D2), consumers will buy 2 million widgets with a price tag of £2 and buy a million even if the price rises to £3.

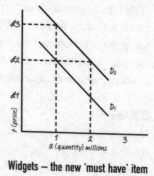

Widgets – the new 'must have' item

SUPPLY

There is another factor influencing the price: how much the widget manufacturer has to charge per item to cover their costs and produce a reasonable profit for shareholders. So the supply curve, going in the opposite

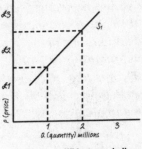

Widget supply lines

direction to the demand curve, shows how many widgets will be supplied at any given price.

In this case, 1 million widgets will be supplied at a price of £1.50 per unit, and 2 million widgets will be supplied if the price is £2.50. Of course, supply curves can move too, especially in response to a change in the price of raw materials.

EQUILIBRIUM

Once the demand and supply curves for widgets are known, both the prevailing price charged and the quantity supplied will be established by the 'equilibrium' point between demand and

supply: in other words, the place where the lines cross. In this case (assuming demand at D1), the answer is that 1.25 million widgets will be sold at a price of £1.75.

But . . .

Of course, it's much

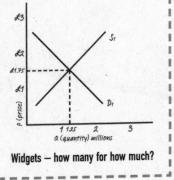

Widgets – how many for how much?

more complicated than this. The textbook models assume perfect information and perfect rationality. In truth, markets are driven by human emotions like greed, fear and hope. If 2008 taught us anything, it taught us this. And don't make the mistake of confusing price and value. The model gives you the price but not necessarily the true value.

CONVER-
SATION

At its core marketing is about showing people how your brand or organization can solve their problems, anticipate their needs, or make their lives better.

The Freeman Company[1]

The problem with the world today is communication. Too much communication.

Homer Simpson

THE RISE AND RISE OF THE PRODUCING CONSUMER

In our experience, the best marketers do not lack bravado. But even they are struggling to project steely self-confidence in the face of profound changes to the world in which they do business.

One of the most visible manifestations of these changes will already be familiar to you – the rise of social media and its cousin, big data analytics. If you have a Sky+ box or Virgin Media's TiVO service, or are a Netflix subscriber, you will already be watching more TV on demand and time-shifting your media consumption.

The year 2015 was important symbolically: it was when the proportion of people preferring to stream TV content (53%) overtook those watching live (45%). Most of those aged between 14 to 25 (Trailing Millennials) now watch more content on mobile devices than they do on actual TVs, according to a study by Deloitte.[2]

When was the last time you spent any serious time watching TV ads? Probably it was some time ago. The old broadcast model route to consumers – the so-called *one-to-many* model of communication – is narrowing by the month. The replacement – so-called *many-to-many* communication – heralds a seismic shift in the power of consumers. Marketing will never be the same again.

The extraordinary growth of smartphone ownership

has fuelled the many-to-many revolution. Smartphones, these new weapons of mass collaboration,[3] allow millions of individuals and communities to create content,[4] share ideas and interests, talk to each other, talk to you, leave recommendations, share networks and causes and build or break brand reputations.

We are no longer passive consumers but are becoming active producers. For some, this shift heralds a genuinely new epoch – the age of mass innovation,[5] in which we are democratizing the production and consumption of everything as we change the way we communicate and share. All of this is having a decisive impact on how companies face their markets and on the very nature of markets themselves.

As a consequence, marketing experts have been quick to proclaim the slow death of cold-calling or the pre-eminence of the 30-second advertising slot,[6] as the disconnect between marketer (sender) and consumer (receiver) increases.[7]

The argument runs that *old marketing* – 'the act of interrupting masses of people with ads about average products' – is being replaced by *new marketing* – 'which leverages scarce attention and creates interactions among communities with similar interests'.[8]

Enterprises are afraid that their increasingly fickle and media-sophisticated consumers are in danger of turning away from them. And they are right to be afraid.

FROM MARKETING TO CONVERSATION

What does all this mean for how businesses reach and influence their customers? In simple terms:

companies, products and markets, and the communities that sustain them, are increasingly built by conversation. If marketing was once the essential differentiator in ensuring that a new product or service met consumer need, it is being usurped by a less controlled and more dynamic interaction between producer and consumer. For all sorts of enterprises, the ability to create new ideas, products, marketing campaigns and opportunities is becoming rooted in their ability to stage new conversations with their markets and their customers.

Conversation is an inherently creative activity. As the writer Theodore Zeldin memorably said, 'When minds meet, they don't just exchange facts; they transform them, reshape them, draw different implications from them, engage in new trains of thought. Conversation does not simply reshuffle the cards. It creates new cards.'[9]

The challenge for marketeers is that their core instinct is to attempt to influence the customer in a *controlled* way. But now success requires a more dynamic, real-time and messy flow of information, ideas and exchange between producer and consumer, in which both parties will change their approach or perception as a result. All of which means it's more important than ever for your marketing activity to be active, not passive.

FROM THE FOUR Ps TO THE FIVE Cs

If the aim of marketing is to satisfy customer needs or wants, how has the discipline traditionally approached this challenge?

The dominant conceptual model underpinning marketing strategy has been the so-called *marketing mix* – which is a generalized model used to describe the different kinds of choices organizations have to make in the whole process of bringing a product or service to market.

The most famous shorthand for those broad choices remains the Four Ps framework, originally proposed by E. Jerome McCarthy, focusing on product, price, place and promotion, which taken together provide the basic components of a marketing plan.[10]

The first two Ps (product and price) are in essence product-related elements. The other two Ps are parts of the delivery system – with 'place' about delivering the physical product or service and 'promotion' about delivering the 'sales messages' and communicating with potential customers.[11]

Different products will produce different points of emphasis, or balance, within the marketing mix. So, for example, within industrial markets more emphasis is usually given to direct contact (involving face-to-face selling), as opposed to the indirect techniques (of marketing research and advertising) used in most consumer markets.[12]

The recent history of marketing has been driven by the partial rejection and ongoing modification of the basic Four Ps model. Marketers have busily been adding extra Ps to the model – like throwing bricks on a failing coastal defence as the tide creeps ever higher.[13] The additional Ps, such as 'people' and 'process', have been added to ensure the model is equally applicable to services as well as product markets.

But the demise of the Four Ps model is a metaphor for the broader collapse of marketing certainties.

The challenge is no longer to adapt existing models, but to accept that the rules of the game have changed – and as a consequence so must the very essence of marketing.

The Four Ps are being taken over by the Five Cs:

- **CONTENT**
- **COMMUNITY**
- **CO-CREATION**
- **CUSTOMIZATION**
- **CONVERSATION**

CONTENT

BRANDED CONTENT AND EXPERIENCE – THE POWER COUPLE OF NEW ERA MARKETING

Marketing has shifted from trying to shout about what your content is to the content itself being the marketing. If you're not preoccupied with content, who you're producing it with, and how it's shared, your marketing strategy is heading south.

'Being able to tell a story in marketing terms is more important than it's ever been. In politics, the phrase "where's the narrative" became a cornerstone of retail offers to the electorate from political parties,' says Simon Burton (a 'marketing guru', according to the *Observer* newspaper). Where's the narrative has now become the DNA of marketing.

Branded content, and the compelling brand experiences that result, are the power couple of new era marketing. The way to cut through the *many-to-many* white noise, and connect with consumers, is by creating content and experiences that in turn creates a lasting relationship between the brand and an individual. Ideally, one that lasts much longer than it takes them to click a pay button or walk to the till.

Branded content experiences can encompass anything from films, events, trade shows, sponsorships, virtual and hybrid events to augmented reality experiences.[14] Compelling content creates an opportunity for a business or charity to engage, converse and create a user-centric, personalized experience. Nine out of ten marketers agree that brand experience delivers strong face-to-face interaction and more compelling brand engagement. More than one in three chief marketing officers expect to set aside 21–50% of their budgets for brand experience development.[15]

Red Bull is the poster child of new era marketing, through its brilliant use of sponsorship activation, experiences and branded content. There are many good accounts of its approach which are worth further reading.[16] Red Bull has tailored its marketing and sponsorship strategy in unique ways, pioneering a new path in sponsorship and marketing for others to follow, sponsoring not only sports-based facets, but also art shows, breakdancing and video-game events. Red Bull's famous tagline – 'Red Bull gives you wings' – animates arresting stories and inspiring events. Slogans such as 'Ever dreamed you could fly?' and 'Ever dreamed of being an astronaut?' got people's attention. Hasn't everybody? So why not buy an energy drink that gives you wings?[17]

The Red Bull Stratos project reached its peak when Austrian skydiver Felix Baumgartner freefell nearly 39,000 metres (128,000 feet) from the edge of space. The jump broke the world record. Huge media attention was generated. A live audience of 8 million people watched the live YouTube stream.[18] As we go to press with this edition, the view count for the company's YouTube video of Baumgartner's freefall stands at nearly 42 million.

Clearly, branded content matters – and is something you need to understand if you're going to connect and converse with a large audience. But there is a broader lesson here too, about the whole picture in terms of the new art of marketing conversation.

What is important is not just what Red Bull has achieved in reach and impact through branded content (they have a 30% share of the global market for energy drinks)[19] – but rather how they have done it.

In particular, they think like a media owner.

You need to think like one too if you're marketing a business, or yourself.

THINK LIKE A MEDIA OWNER – BECAUSE YOU ARE ONE

Simon Burton argues that we are all, both businesses and individuals, media owners now, Counter-intuitive? Only if you are thinking with an 'old media' mindset.

If you have Facebook friends and Twitter followers, you're a media owner. If your Twitter account has 10,000 followers, you're already a niche magazine in terms of reach and draw. What do you mean you don't have an editorial policy and tone of voice for your brand? If you don't, the art of underselling yourself is clearly alive and well.

Businesses are almost by definition powerful media owners. It is just that many haven't realized it yet. They are so bad at conversing with their

Have we got your attention yet?
Felix Baumgartner's freefall from 128,000 feet

markets they're in the equivalent of a commercial circulation crisis.

Back to Red Bull. They act and think more like a media owner than an energy drinks business. Let's do a checklist:

- THEY ARE A FULLY-FLEDGED PUBLISHER WITH A RANGE OF CONTENT PRODUCTS AND CHANNELS[20] ☑
- THEY HAVE A CLEAR STRATEGY FOR CONTENT AND EXPERIENCE PROPERTIES THAT RESONATE DEEPLY WITH THEIR TARGET AUDIENCES ☑
- THEY SEEK TO OWN PROPERTIES (RED BULL AIR RACE; RED BULL RACING) AND THE CONTENT AND REVENUE STREAMS THAT FLOW FROM THEM ☑
- THEY'RE DIGITAL AND MOBILE FIRST[21] ☑

They also have a good recipe and processes to make an energy drink, but a 30% global market share for their product category has been achieved through their media ownership behaviour and the resulting compelling content and customer connection, not because their canning plant rocks.

In contrast, many brands are stuck in the weeds of poor communication and projection. What are the symptoms? Sending out salesy emails or annoying customers with banner ads are early stage indicators. As John Hall, *Forbes* contributor, asks, somewhat acidly: 'When was the last time you clicked on a banner ad? What about the last time you listened to a telemarketer's entire spiel and then whipped out your credit card to book a cruise?'

AND THROUGH THE STORIES WE TELL, WE PROVOKE CONVERSATIONS

Consumers have become adept in skipping overt sales pitches in search of the data and resources they need to form an opinion. To make his case, Hall highlights a recent study by *Ad Age* revealing that 75% of marketers have got the wrong idea about content marketing. In the survey, 75% of marketers said content should frequently mention products and services (despite the fact that 60% of their audience turns down overtly sales-y content).[22]

Instead, think content and act like a media owner. Follow Coca Cola's lead, with their Content 2020 initiative, their content advertising strategy from storytelling to content creation. Coca Cola's model starts with brand stories designed to provoke conversations with customers to produce ideas, that they then seek to act on, and react to, 365 days a year. The aim is to earn 'a *disproportionate share of popular culture*'. They sound a lot like a media owner, and a storyteller. To us, the whole approach sounds a lot like marketing as conversation.

COMMUNITY – FRIEND OR FOE?

The second big challenge for traditional marketing is that success is no longer just about enlisting individual consumers, but about how best to engage the communities in which they hang out, hunt and harangue. Consumption, it appears, really is best served in a crowd.[23]

Aided and abetted by the internet and social media, which simultaneously allow us to find our tribes and communities, consumption is increasing a social or peer-led activity.

As Philip Kotler and colleagues note: 'Recent research across industries show that most customers believe more in the f-factor (friends, families, Facebook fans, Twitter followers) than in marketing communications . . . It is as if customers were protecting themselves from false brand claims by using their social circles to build a fortress.'[24] For companies, this means consumers aren't targets to be hit with outbound messaging, rather peers to be invited into a conversation that might interest them about a given brand, or product or service – through compelling content, not sales coercion.

The problem for companies is that as consumers, and the tribes they run in, have become more valuable, they have also become more vengeful. They quickly call out or dismiss bad service or crass marketing messages and targeting. Both these attributes demand that enterprises should seek to be in constant conversation with them. Not an easy task now that everyone is a media owner and companies have no control over the conversation. As Kotler says: 'Marketers need to create brand conversations in customer communities despite not having much control over the outcome.'

Some of those conversations are with individuals who are their biggest friends and fans – they're people who love them already. The challenge then is how to amplify their contribution and voice.

But some conversations are with their biggest foes. They've been burned by a bad product or poor customer service and they're intent on flaming the reputation of the offending company. Enterprises must work even harder to stay in the conversation game with them, but to a different end – to get them to change their pitch or their tone or, better still, to get them to talk about something else altogether.

And as BrandIndex scores reveal (see below), not everybody has to love you for you to be a successful brand, but you do have to be a conversational, proactive brand to keep your friend and foe communities in balance.

'HATERS GONNA HATE' – THAT'S OKAY IF 'LOVERS GONNA LOVE'

In his book Marketing 4.0 *Kotler gives a nice example of how strong consumer advocacy for a brand often needs to be activated by either customer enquiries or negative advocacy. Great* brands do not necessarily have significantly more lovers than haters. According to YouGov's BrandIndex, McDonald's, for example, has 33% lovers and 29% haters. Starbucks has a similar profile: 30% lovers and 23% haters. What should you make of this? Perhaps your brand's lovers and haters are looming large in your marketplace. Should you be focusing your efforts on one set over the other? Here is what Kotler and his co-authors advise (and we agree):

'From the Net Promoter Score point of view, two of the biggest brands in the food and beverage industry would have very low scores because they have too many haters. But from an alternative viewpoint, the group of haters is a necessary evil that activates the group of lovers to defend McDonald's and Starbucks against criticisms. Without both positive and negative advocacy, the brand conversations would be dull and less engaging.

'Any brand that has strong characters and DNA would likely be unpopular with a certain market segment. But what these brands should aim to have is the ultimate sales force: an army of lovers who are willing to guard the brand in the digital world.'

How's your army of lovers coming on?

Are you doing anything to actively recruit and nurture them?

Some major brands go as far as to 'poke' the haters to get a reaction, creating a conversation and getting their supporters to defend their product. The aim being that fans might sway neutral consumers into becoming supporters (on the assumption that most of the haters are lost to the brand already). Ryanair, the discount airline well known to European readers, has long needled critics of its no-frills service by making tongue-in-cheek proposals for new ways to trim amenities.[26] One of Ryanair's more notorious suggestions was the introduction of a 'fat tax'. In 2009, the budget airline ran an online competition giving customers the chance to win free flights by coming up with novel ideas to save or make the company money. Around 100,000 passengers took part in the online competition and of those 30,000 (29%) voted for a fee for overweight passengers. In a classic 'dead cat strategy', Ryanair never brought in this policy, and the only change they made was the removal of some toilets (which seems 'reasonable' by comparison), an announcement made only after their provocative kite-flying of the 'fat tax' had put the company firmly in the headlines and in lots of people's conversations.[27]

But energizing your fans and enhancing word-of-mouth marketing is only one benefit of getting the conversation right with your consumers. The biggest prize of all awaits those companies who can turn them into *prosumers* – consumers who help create the products, services, content and campaigns they themselves want to use, shape and take part in.[28] This is the vision of consumer as producer and co-creator.

CO-CREATION

Firms can no longer create stories, meaning and value in splendid isolation. Value is increasingly being co-created by the firm and the consumer, as consumers actively help design, develop and distribute the products and services they value and the marketing campaigns that get people talking about the product or service. Twenty-five percent of search results for the world's 20 largest brands are now linked to user-generated content, according to Kissmetrics. And brand engagements rise by 28% when consumers are exposed to both professional content and user-generated product video (comScore).[29]

Co-created marketing works, and many campaigns now have co-creation baked in – with Facebook pages, hashtags and digital reach allowing brands to create opportunities for their fans to chime in, create content and build the story about the brand.

For companies, the attraction of co-creating is that user-generated elements of campaigns can enrich the campaign story by showing what the product, the brand or the messages mean to the people who use it every day. At best, these user-generated stories and campaigns can feel more authentic, and have more positive viral possibilities, than anything a corporate marketing department could dream up in isolation.

A vivid example was provided by Airbnb in 2013, when the firm created the first short film made entirely of Vines sent in by users from all over the world (the resulting film is on http://blog.atairbnb.com/airbnb-presents-hollywood-vines/). The film, which is a wistful account of the journey of a single piece of paper, was created from instructions sent out by the company to their Twitter fans, and was a clever piece of story-telling content for the travel company.

Certain demographics seem particularly attracted to the magic of user-generated content, in particular the millennial generation, who have grown up digital. In 2014, Crowdtap and Ipsos Media CT released a survey showing how popular and trusted user-generated content is for millennials. The study found that millennials spend a staggering 18 hours per day consuming different media across several devices. User-generated content makes up 30% of that time (5.4 hours), second only to traditional media like print, television and radio at 33%. Millennials trust information found in user-generated content 50% more than information from traditional media sources and find user-generated content 35% more memorable than other sources.[30]

So if your users aren't part of your storytelling team about your brand, you're going to find it harder to make it feel personal and trusted. As Mark Bonchek and colleagues note: 'Everybody likes to talk about being "customer-centric." But too often this means taking better aim with targeted campaigns. Customers today are not just consumers; they are also creators, developing content and ideas – and encountering challenges – right along with you.'[31]

This scrambling of the marketing value chain reflects the heightened desire of consumers to play with and shape the things they care about. But it also, rather paradoxically, makes innovation potentially more manageable. The big risk in new product and service innovation for companies is that they fail to anticipate correctly how consumers will respond to and use their new market offerings. Consumer-driven innovation and co-creation diminishes these risks, as consumers actively design products and services to meet their wants and needs. Moreover, they often create new markets and sources of value as a consequence,[32] displaying their ability to move beyond a traditional, passive consumption of ideas and goods to co-creating and owning content or products.[33]

For example, LEGO has long seen the value in co-creating products with customers (both young and old). Any idea what this is?

It's a MINDSTORMS® robot made by LEGO® Group.

When the product first made its debut in 1989, LEGO® Group's marketers were surprised to discover that the robotic toys were popular not only with teenagers, the envisaged market, but also with adult hobbyists eager to improve them.

Adult hobbyists. That's a descriptive phrase to conjure with. We mean geeks – people who live with their heads inside computers, wearing slogan T-shirts, looking longingly at screens and creating unimaginative profiles (they're geeks, remember) on internet dating sites. But they're a market – and a much more lucrative market than LEGO® Group ever imagined. Within weeks of releasing the product, MINDSTORMS® robot communities had sprung up who had hacked into the electronics, reprogrammed the robots and then began to send their suggested improvements to LEGO® Group.

LEGO® Group's response?

They threatened legal action – the conversational equivalent of a slamming door, only less eloquent.

As their consumers rebelled, with fans turning into foes, eventually LEGO® Group came round. It embraced the hacker community – about to become MINDSTORMS's® biggest fans and backers – and wrote a 'right to hack' into the MINDSTORMS® software licence, giving hobbyists explicit permission to let their imaginations run wild.

That was the starting point for LEGO to transform itself into a co-creation company, which now has a permanent co-creation platform for its fans and users. LEGO Ideas is its online community where members can see and review new creations by other fans and submit their own designs for new sets. Fans can vote on submissions and give feedback. If a project gets 10,000 votes, LEGO reviews the idea and picks a winner for an official LEGO Ideas set to be created and sold worldwide. The creator gives final product approval, earns a percentage of the

sales and is recognized as the creator on all packaging and marketing. This concept celebrates loyal customers and rewards them for innovation, creativity and entrepreneurialism.[34]

The favourite design of one of the authors of this book, which met the 10,000 vote threshold, is the VW Golf MK1 GTI.[35] It would take too long to properly explain why, but for UK readers, he's an Essex boy in mid-life. *Capisce*? The other author used Lego bricks to demonstrate barriers to inter-generational mobility for, at last count, 400,000 YouTube viewers.[36]

CUSTOMIZATION

Content, community and co-creation are all vital in supporting and driving customization, another vital part of the new marketing mix. In the digital era, where companies are collecting copious amounts of real-time data about their customers, marketers have an enhanced ability to understand, predict and customize customers' experiences. As Caren Fleit notes: 'Big data and artificial intelligence swamp marketers with information. The focus shifts from telling and selling to customer engagement and dialogues and personalized communications and products.'[37]

Happily for marketers, the opportunities for customization have never been greater. The rise of ever more sophisticated customer relationship management (CRM) systems, big data and predictive analytical tools mean that by analyzing and listening better, and understanding consumer behaviour across all the touch points they have with a business, companies can use their social CRM approach to provide customized and tailored recommendations and solutions. In other words, next generation customer service and marketing – intuitive, proactive and personalized (see below).

How can you best respond to these developments? We noted earlier that companies need to think of themselves as media owners to market their products and services successfully. They also need to think of themselves as data companies, whether they are a retailer, manufacturer or service provider. One way to understand where marketing and customization are heading is to look at Walmart.

In case you hadn't noticed, Walmart has been reinventing itself as a data company to drive its retail business.[38] It now describes itself as follows: 'We're not a retailer competing in Silicon Valley. We're building an internet technology company inside the world's largest retailer.'[39] At the heart of this reinvention is social data - tweets, blogs, pins, comments, shares and so on. All of that data is analysed by WalmartLabs to generate retail-related insights. Their key project has been the Social Genome project – which they define as 'a giant knowledge base that captures entities and relationships of the social world'. Walmart has spent the last few years building this in-house Social Genome, part public data, part private data, with a vast array of social media data streaming into it. Streaming in so fast that WalmartLabs created something they call Muppet, a solution for processing Fast Data using large clusters of machines.[40]

The big data team at WalmartLabs is the customer-focused nerve centre of the business. It analyses every clickable action on Walmart.com: what consumers buy in-store and online; what is trending on Twitter, local events such as the San Francisco

Giants winning the World Series, and how local weather deviations affect buying patterns. All the events are captured and analysed intelligently by big data algorithms to discern meaningful big data insights for the millions of customers so that Walmart can then craft a personalized shopping experience for each of them.[41] For the customer that means they get ever more relevant personal offers, notifications and invitations. Groups of consumers interested in a particular new fad or fashion find that Walmart has anticipated the forthcoming demand and stocked their stores in anticipation.

For example, in 2011, the team correctly anticipated heightened customer interest in cake-pop makers based on social media conversations on Facebook and Twitter. A few months later, it noticed growing interest in electric juicers, linked in part to the popularity of the juice-crazy documentary *Fat, Sick and Nearly Dead*. The team sends this data to Walmart's buyers, who then use it to make their purchasing decisions.[42]

Walmart's public commentary on the initiative has declined since launch. Our instinct is that this is less about its declining influence on Walmart's marketing, sales and revenue. Rather, it is that the insights and competitive advantage being secured by Walmart is becoming too valuable to widely share, and they don't want to alarm consumers who currently enjoy Walmart's personalized marketing and retail offers, but might be a lot shyer about being in conversation with them as a customer if they knew just how much Walmart now knows about them and can accurately predict about their future behaviour.

So, is consumer customization at the heart of your

business? Are you thinking strategically as a data-driven business? Are you doing everything you can to understand and anticipate the needs and preferences of your customers?

SOCIAL MEDIA MARKETING REQUIRES SMART SOCIAL LISTENING. IT'S NOT A CONVERSATION WITHOUT IT

When customers have a good or bad experience they increasingly share it with everyone.

So, social media monitoring, listening and responding (social relationship management) are crucial in allowing a company to tap in quickly to customer complaints, compliments or concerns and react quickly.

You might be thinking this seems almost too obvious to note – but you'd be surprised how many companies don't systematically monitor social channels, or perhaps worse, monitor but don't respond quickly or appropriately, and therefore are seen not to be listening – or keen to be in conversation. Some 72% of people who complain to a brand on Twitter expect an answer within an hour. Yet Twitter data shows that nearly 40% of customers tweets never get a response from the company. And recent McKinsey analysis shows that 30% of social media users prefer 'social care' to phoning customer service.[43]

It is therefore vital that your omni-channel approach to customer contact and interaction is up to scratch. For example, effective social CRM helps organizations generate leads by solving problems, attracts new customers, improves customer care, identifies influences and advocates, and drives innovation.[44]

Companies that do social CRM well, in a customized, non-invasive and relevant way, improved year-over-year revenue per contact by 6.7% (those that didn't saw a corresponding 12.1% decline).[45]

And some consumers may be willing to share more of their data in return for customization. A recent study found that 22% of consumers are happy to share some data in return for a more personalized customer service or product.[46]

Evidence suggests that a company's social CRM and listening loops break down when they treat social media as a siloed part of their communications strategy, or something 'that's done by their marketing department, rather than the most crucial way they have of getting close to people and communicating what it is they do'.[47]

CONVERSATION

The final C is conversation. Marketers have long claimed that they are the generator of the customer-eye view of any business, stressing that their over-riding mission is to engage with their customers as much as possible in as many different ways as possible.

Maybe – marketers have never lacked a sales pitch, after all. But those companies clinging to the certainties of old marketing models won't deliver on this mission. The Five Cs are rapidly undermining the core of almost all traditional marketing theory. Content, community, customization and co-creation are eroding the gap between marketing on one side and the customer on the other.

As one expert puts it: 'It's not us and them. It's us and us.'[48]

Customers have more power than ever before and they've changed. Marketers are going to have to change with them – and use the Five Cs to enable the most important C of them all, the art of conversation. Most marketers already recognize they're now in the conversation business. Many also need to accept that they urgently need elocution lessons. They'll soon be talking to markets differently as they're always looking for an edge, and marketers haven't given up hope that they might yet be able to read customers' minds.

NEUROMARKETING

The influential British economist Lionel Robbins declared that it was not possible to 'peer into men's minds' to discover their true desires. But that was three-quarters of a century ago. Now we are peering in earnest. A fast-growing subdiscipline of neurology and marketing, neuromarketing, *represents a terrifically exciting scientific advance into the understanding of consumer behaviour – or a totally terrifying Orwellian development, depending on your point of view. The word itself was coined in 2002, but the discipline has only recently begun to take off.*

Subjects are placed in MRI scanners while

they look at images, or attached to mobile brain-imaging machines while they shop. Then neuroscientists can see what happens to their brains when they buy something, see a brand name they recognize, or swallow a mouthful of a soft drink. The most famous example is a high-tech version of the 'Coke versus Pepsi' challenge.

The findings from Samuel McClure and his colleagues were startling. When people did not know what they were drinking, roughly half said they preferred each brand. The subjects' ventromedial prefrontal cortex – essentially the brain's feel-good centre – was actually more strongly activated by Pepsi than Coke.

But when the guinea pigs knew what they were drinking, the scans revealed activity in the hippocampus, midbrain and dorsolateral prefrontal cortex: areas associated with memory and feelings.

Here is what the re-searchers concluded: 'Subjects in this part of the experiment preferred Coke in the labelled cups significantly more than Coke in the anonymous tasks . . . We hypothesize that cultural information biases preference decisions through the dorsolateral region of the prefrontal cortex, with the hippocampus engaged to recall the associated information.'

To you and me: such is the power of Coke's brand that people do not merely think they prefer it to Pepsi. They actually do prefer it, so long as they know what they're drinking.[49]

A powerful scientific testimony to the enduring power of a brand.

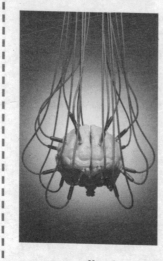

Unsurprisingly interest and investment in neuromarketing techniques are strengthening, with lots of next wave innovation predicted around eye-tracking and facial encoding (particularly as AI and machine learning progammes start to automatically 'read' and interpret our facial expressions (what we are really thinking) and our text and vocal exchanges with a service provider.[50]

THANK YOU FOR YOUR 80 MINUTES.

GENERAL RESOURCES

We hope that this book makes you more business curious – not just in terms of searching out the key texts and references that we direct you to in each of our individual chapter resources and references sections, but also in terms of how best to make use of a wide range of additional print and online materials.

EDITED BOOKS AND COLLECTIONS

A number of the key business schools produce excellent summary series covering key business and management issues. See for example the *Harvard Business Review* Paperback series, which features highly readable collections of seminal essays from the review grouped by theme – such as marketing, leadership and corporate social responsibility (www.hbsp.harvard.edu).

LEADING BUSINESS SCHOOLS IN THE UK AND GLOBALLY

Almost all of the leading business schools now provide freely downloadable podcasts or videos, featuring lectures by their main teaching faculty or other guest expert speakers. The podcasts cover both key elements of an MBA syllabus and also key topical issues.

For example, Wharton has 2 million subscribers to its journal Knowledge@Wharton, which is published in multiple languages (http://knowledge.wharton.upenn.edu/).

London Business School has an excellent YouTube channel, like most of the major business schools. For example, see this great companion to the Leadership and Culture sections, a lecture given by Professor Gareth Jones on 'Why Should Anyone Work Here' https://www.youtube.com/watch?v=DM2QVuHpfKE.

In a similar vein, the Massachusetts Institute of Technology (MIT) and its Sloan Management School, have their own YouTube channel with a huge variety of great lectures and videos (https://www.youtube.com/channel/UCKgamS4zSNmq7r7tQB6niLw).

More broadly, a wide range of leading universities from around the globe are now using the iTunes platform, specifically the iTunes University (www.apple.com/itunesu), to distribute podcasts of expert lecture and teaching materials. Apple is effectively creating a global lecture theatre for the engaged *80 Minute MBA* student. For example, Oxford University has its own dedicated iTunes U offer (https://www.ox.ac.uk/itunes-u?wssl=1).

The UK-based Open University has a huge variety of materials available on iTunes University, including a dedicated strand of business and management lectures (http://www.open.edu/itunes/subjects/business-and-management).

If *The 80 Minute MBA* encourages you to pursue just some of these brilliant knowledge resources, not only will the time spent reading this book be doubly worthwhile, but we can be even more confident that future UK managers and leaders are displaying the required level of intellectual curiosity.

Given this proliferation of content providers, where should you start your search? An obvious source of guidance is the annual global MBA ranking, published by the *Financial Times*. The top ten schools in the FT Global MBA Ranking 2017, which would be an excellent place to start to search for relevant materials, were as follows:

- INSEAD - www.insead.edu
- STANFORD UNIVERSITY – www.gsb.stanford.edu
- UNIVERSITY OF PENNSYLVANIA, WHARTON – www.wharton.upenn.edu
- HARVARD BUSINESS SCHOOL – www.hbs.edu
- UNIVERSITY OF CAMBRIDGE, JUDGE – https://www.jbs.cam.ac.uk/home/
- LONDON BUSINESS SCHOOL – www.london.edu
- COLUMBIA BUSINESS SCHOOL – http://www8.gsb.columbia.edu/
- IE BUSINESS SCHOOL – www.ie.edu
- UNIVERSITY OF CHICAGO – https://www.chicagobooth.edu
- IESE BUSINESS SCHOOL – http://www.iese.edu/en/index-default.html

---

PROFESSIONAL ASSOCIATIONS, THINK TANKS AND CONSULTING FIRMS IN THE UK

A wide range of professional associations, think tanks and consulting firms are active in producing research reports and expert commentary on business and management issues. In terms of professional bodies, useful material is provided by:

- **THE CHARTERED MANAGEMENT INSTITUTE** – www.managers.org.uk
- **THE CHARTERED INSTITUTE OF PERSONNEL AND DEVELOPMENT** – https://www.cipd.co.uk
- **THE CHARTERED INSTITUTE OF MARKETING** – www.cim.co.uk
- **THE INSTITUTE OF CHARTERED ACCOUNTANTS IN ENGLAND AND WALES** – www.icaew.com

Professional service firms in the United Kingdom, particularly the so-called 'Big Four' – Pricewater-houseCoopers (PwC), Deloitte Touche Tohmatsu Ltd, Ernst & Young (E&Y) and Klynveld Peat Marwick Goerdeler (KPMG) – remain a useful additional resource for free public domain reports on key aspects of management and business practice. In addition to briefing papers on key industry sectors, they regularly survey CEOs and CFOs on their perspectives and priorities and produce research and reports on key management disciplines and challenges. They also provide a wide range of podcasts on topical issues.

Website addresses are:

- PRICEWATERHOUSECOOPERS — www.pwc.co.uk
- DELOITTE TOUCHE TOHMATSU —
  https://www2.deloitte.com/uk/en.html
- ERNST & YOUNG — http://www.ey.com/uk/en/home
- KPMG — www.kpmg.co.uk

There are also numerous specialist business think tanks providing useful resources across the gamut of MBA issues. Useful institutions in the UK and US include:

- THE INSTITUTE FOR FISCAL STUDIES — www.ifs.org.uk
- THE SOCIAL MARKET FOUNDATION — http://www.smf.co.uk
- INSTITUTE FOR PUBLIC POLICY RESEARCH —
  http://www.ippr.org
- POLICY EXCHANGE — https://policyexchange.org.uk
- THE ROYAL SOCIETY FOR THE ARTS —
  https://www.thersa.org
- NESTA — www.nesta.org.uk
- SUSTAINABILITY — www.sustainability.com
- PETERSON INSTITUTE FOR INTERNATIONAL ECONOMICS —
  https://piie.com
- BROOKINGS INSTITUTION — http://brookings.edu
- CENTER FOR CLIMATE AND ENERGY SOLUTIONS —
  https://www.c2es.org
- INTER-AMERICAN DIALOGUE — http://www.thedialogue.org

And of course, in a world of user-generated content and conversation, if you search a little you will find interesting, curated lists of TED talks relevant to the themes in this book. For example, http://blog.movingworlds.org/the-ted-talk-mba/#business curates under an MBA rubric 143 TED Talks covering essential theories, skills, and concepts taught at leading MBA programs. It was designed by MovingWorlds.org to help people become more globally and socially conscious leaders. Or perhaps see the blog http://blog.event2mobile.com/10-brilliant-ted-talks-that-can-teach-you-more-than-your-mba-in-hr/ offering 10 Brilliant TED Talks That Can Teach You More Than Your MBA in HR – some of them are very much worth watching.

BIBLIO-
GRAPHY

BIBLIO-
GRAPHY

Ahonen, T. T. and Moore, A. (2005) *Communities Dominate Brands: Business and Marketing Challenges for the 21st Century*, Futuretext

Anderson, C. (2006) *The Long Tail: How Endless Choice is Creating Unlimited Demand*, Random House Business Books

Barrow, P. and Epstein, L. (2007) *Bookkeeping for Dummies*, John Wiley & Sons

Bossidy, L. and Charan, R. (2002) *Execution: The Discipline of Getting Things Done*, Crown Business

Broughton, Philip Delves (2008) *What They Teach You at Harvard Business School: My Two Years Inside the Cauldron of Capitalism*, Penguin

Collins, J. and Porras, J. I. (2004) *Built to Last: Successful Habits of Visionary Companies*, Collins Business

Eastaway, R. and Wyndham, J. (2005) *Why do Buses Come in Threes?: The Hidden Mathematics of Everyday Life*, Portico Books

El-Erian, M. (2008) *When Markets Collide: Investment Strategies for the Age of Global Economic Change*, McGraw Hill

Fallon, P. and Senn, F. (2006) *Juicing the Orange:*

How to Turn Creativity into a Powerful Business Advantage, Harvard Business School Press

Friedman, Thomas L. (2008) *Hot, Flat and Crowded*, Farrar, Straus and Giroux

Friedman, Thomas L. (2006) *The World is Flat*, Farrar, Straus and Giroux

Godin, Seth (2007) *Meatball Sundae: How New Marketing is Transforming the Business World*, Piatkus Books

Godin, Seth (2006) *Small is the New Big*, Penguin Business Books

Goffee, R. and Jones, G. (2006) *Why Should Anyone be Led by You?*, Harvard Business School Press

Gore, Al (2006) *An Inconvenient Truth: The Planetary Emergency of Global Warming and What We Can Do About It*, Bloomsbury Publishing

Hand, J. and Lev, B. (eds) (2003) *Intangible Assets: Values, Measures and Risks*, Oxford University Press

Jaffe, Joseph (2007) *Join the Conversation: How to Engage Marketing-Weary Consumers with the Power of Community, Dialogue, and Partnership*, John Wiley & Sons

Jaffe, Joseph (2005) *Life After the 30-Second Spot: Energize Your Brand with a Bold Mix of Alternatives to Traditional Advertising*, John Wiley & Sons

Jenkins, H. (2008) *Convergence Culture: Where Old and New Media Collide*, New York University Press

Keough, Donald R. (2008) *The Ten Commandments for Business Failure*, Penguin Business

Kotler, Philip and Deller, Keven (2008) *Marketing Management*, thirteenth edition, Pearson Education

Leadbeater, C. (2008) *We-Think: Mass Innovation, Not Mass Production*, Profile Books

Lessig, Lawrence (2008) *Remix: Making Art and Commerce Thrive in the Hybrid Economy*, Penguin

Lev, B. (2001) *Intangibles: Management, Measurement, and Reporting*, Brookings Institute

Locke, C. et al (2000) *The Cluetrain Manifesto: The End of Business as Usual*, Perseus Books

Lynas, Mark (2008) *Six Degrees: Our Future on a Hotter Planet*, Harper Perennial

McCarthy, E. J. (1981) *Basic Marketing: A Managerial Approach*, Richard D. Irwin

Mercer, David (1995) *Marketing*, second edition, Wiley-Blackwell

Paulos, John Allen (1996) *A Mathematician Reads the Newspapers*, Anchor Books

Paulos, John Allen (2001) *Innumeracy: Mathematical Illiteracy and its Consequences*, Hill & Wang

Penn, Mark J. (2007) *Micro Trends: Surprising Tales of the Way We Live Today*, Penguin

Pine, J. II, (1992) *Mass Customization: The New Frontier in Business Competition*, Harvard Business School Press

Porter, Michael (2004) *Competitive Advantage*, Free Press

Porter, Michael (2004) *Competitive Strategy: Techniques for Analyzing Industries and Competitors*, Free Press

Raymond, Martin (2003) *The Tomorrow People: Future Consumers and How to Read Them Today*, FT Prentice Hall

Shiller, R. J. (2008) *The Subprime Solution: How Today's Global Financial Crisis Happened, and What to Do about It*, Princeton University Press

Shirky, Clay (2008) *Here Comes Everybody: The Power of Organizing without Organizations*, Allen Lane

Spencer, L. Vaughan (2008) *Don't Be Needy Be Succeedy*, Profile Books

Stern, Nicholas (2007) *The Economics of Climate Change: The Stern Review*, Cambridge University Press

Tapscott, D. and Williams, A. D. (2006) *Wikinomics: How Mass Collaboration Changes Everything*, Atlantic Books

Wood, F. and Robinson, S. (2004) *Book-Keeping and Accounts*, FT Prentice Hall

Zeldin, T. (2000) *Conversation: How Talk Can Change Our Lives*, Hidden Spring

NOTES

NOTES

INTRODUCTION

1 http://www.edelman.com/news/2017-edelman-trust-barometer-reveals-global-implosion/

2 Henry Mintzberg, 'Scrap the MBA', https://hbr.org/2009/04/audio-scrap-the-mba-or-no-titl

3 Schoemaker, P. (2008) *The Future Challenges of Business: Rethinking Management Education*, Case Study, Harvard Business Review, https://hbr.org/product/the-future-challenges-of-business-rethinking-management-education/CMR399-PDF-ENG. See also McDonald, D. (2017), *The Golden Passport: Harvard Business School, the Limits of Capitalism and the Moral Failure of the MBA Elite*, HarperBusiness

4 McDonald, D. 'The "Golden Passport" is Stamped with Hubris', *The Times*, 3 June 2017, https://www.thetimes.co.uk/article/the-golden-passport-is-stamped-with-hubris-tx-bz52mw3

5 Bianchi, E. and Mohliver, A., 'CEOs Who Began Their Careers During Booms Tend to Be Less Ethical', *Harvard Business Review*, 12 May 2017, https://hbr.org/2017/05/ceos-who-began-their-careers-during-booms-tend-to-be-less-ethical

6 See Shiller, R. J. (2008) *The Subprime Solution: How Today's Global Financial Crisis Happened, and What to Do about It*, Princeton University Press

SUSTAINABILITY

1 Berners-Lee, M. and Clark, D. (2013) *The Burning Question: We Can't Burn Half the World's Oil, Coal and Gas. So How Do We Quit?*, Profile Books; see also their useful set of resources at http://www.burningquestion.info

2 See https://corporate.marksandspencer.com/documents/plan-a/plan-a-2025-commitments.pdf

3 See Omond, Tamsin (2009) *Rush! The Making of a Climate Activist*, Marion Boyars

4 See http://www.independent.co.uk/news/world/google-renewable-energy-2016-carbon-neutral-climate-change-amazon-microsoft-a7460281.html

5 Lynas, Mark, *Six Degrees: Our Future on a Hotter Planet* (2009), Fourth Estate

6 See: https://www.wired.com/2016/12/global-warming-beneath-permafrost/

7 Data taken from http://www.gallup.com/poll/206030/global-warming-concern-three-decade-high.aspx

8 Mario Molina, 'Don't Gamble with our Climate Future', news story, http://news.mit.edu/2015/compton-lecture-mario-molina-climate-change-0513

9 See http://www.acclimatise.uk.com/resources?resource=261; and https://environmentagency.blog.gov.uk/2014/06/23/becoming-climate-ready-business-resilience-in-a-changing-climate/

10 http://www.popsci.com/science/article/2012-01/maldivian-leaders-are-buying-foreign-land-future-climate-refugees

11 http://www.cisl.cam.ac.uk/business-action/low-carbon-transformation/ipcc-climate-science-business-briefings/pdfs/briefings/IPCC_AR5__Implications_for_Tourism__Briefing__WEB_EN.pdf

12 https://www.ft.com/content/16d888d4-f790-11e3-b2cf-00144feabdc0

13 See http://www.ey.com/Publication/vwLUAssets/EY-climate-change-and-investment/$FILE/EY-climate-change-and-investment.pdf

14 http://www.carbontracker.org/resources/

15 'Barclays: German Coal "Worthless" by 2030', cleanenergywire.org, 18 March 2016

16 Dietz, S., Bowen, A., Dixon, C. and Gradwell, P., '"Climate Value at Risk" of Global Financial Assets', *Nature Climate Change*, April 2016 (http://www.nature.com/nclimate/journal/v6/n7/full/nclimate2972.html?WT.feed_name=subjects_environmental-economics&foxtrotcallback=true); 'The Cost of Inaction', The Economist Intelligence Unit, July 2015

17 From http://www.ey.com/Publication/vwLUAssets/EY-climate-change-and-investment/$FILE/EY-climate-change-and-investment.pdf

18 Dawkins, R., 'Sustainability Doesn't Come Naturally: A

Darwinian Perspective on Values', Inaugural Lecture on the Value Platform for Sustainability, The Environment Foundation, 2001 (bitly.com/darwins-talk)

19 Berners-Lee and Clark, *The Burning Question,* op cit

20 http://www.fao.org/news/story/en/item/197608/icode/

21 https://www.theguardian.com/sustainable-business/2015/may/05/millennials-employment-employers-values-ethics-jobs

22 http://www.experian.co.uk/blogs/latest-thinking/benefits-going-green-company

23 https://www.businessgreen.com/digital_assets/8779/hsbc_Stranded–assets–what–next.pdf

24 https://www.greenbiz.com/article/will-frances-corporate-climate-reporting-model-go-global

25 https://www.wemeanbusinesscoalition.org/sites/default/files/BECC_Business-Summary_0.pdf

26 https://www.wemeanbusinesscoalition.org/sites/default/files/BECC–Business-Summary–0.pdf

27 Hawken, P. (2017) *Drawdown: The Most Comprehensive Plan Ever Proposed to Roll Back Global Warming,* Penguin; and https://www.vox.com/energy-and-environment/2017/5/10/15589038/top-100-solutions-climate-change-ranked

28 'Why Microsoft gave Sustainability a Promotion', Greenbiz, 14 March 2016, https://www.greenbiz.com/article/why-microsoft-gave-sustainability-promotion

Also worth reading are:

New China, 'Global Warming Heats Up Extreme Weather, Deteriorates Environment: Nobel laureate', http://news.xinhuanet.com/english/2017-05/09/c_136266872.htm; Dieter Helm (2012) *The Carbon Crunch: How We're Getting Climate Change Wrong – and How to Fix It,* Yale University Press; Naomi Oreskes and Erik Conway (2010) *Merchants of Doubt: How a Handful of Scientists Obscured the Truth on Issues from Tobacco Smoke to Global Warming,* Bloomsbury Press; and Mark Lynas (2009) *Six Degrees: Our Future on a Hotter Planet,* Fourth Estate.

There is an excellent interview with Paul Hawken about how in averting climate change we need to focus of course on energy and fossil fuels, but also more on solutions which combine two key ingredients – agency and affordability. See https://www.vox.com/energy-and-environment/2017/5/10/15589038/top-100-

solutions-climate-change-ranked. See also 'Climate Change: The Investment Perpsective', http://www.ey.com/Publication/vwLU Assets/EY-climate-change-and-investment/$FILE/EY-climate-change-and-investment.pdf.

For the UK government's latest risk assessment on the impact of climate change on the UK, see https://www.gov.uk/government/uploads/system/uploads/attachment_data/file/584281/uk-climate-change-risk-assess-2017.pdf

LEADERSHIP

1 Wallace, David Foster (2005) *Consider the Lobster: And Other Essays*, Abacus

2 https://serveleadnow.com/why-are-there-so-many-leadership-books/

3 https://hbr.org/ideacast/2016/01/stop-focusing-on-your-strengths.html

4 Richard Kovacevic in Pfeffer, Jeffrey (1998) *The Human Equation*', Harvard Business School Press

5 Favaro, Ken, 'Defining Strategy, Implementation, and Execution', *Harvard Business Review*, 31 March 2015, https://hbr.org/2015/03/defining-strategy-implementation-and-execution

6 Leinwand, Paul and Mainarid, Cesare, 'What Drives a Company's Success?', *Harvard Business Review* (2013)

7 Anthony, Scott, 'What the Media Industry Can Teach Us about Digital Business Models', *Harvard Business Review*, 10 June 2015, https://hbr.org/2015/06/what-the-media-industry-can-teach-us-about-digital-business-models

8 https://www.worldfinance.com/strategy/the-blame-game

9 Goleman, Daniel, 'The Focused Leader', *Harvard Business Review* (2013), https://hbr.org/2013/12/the-focused-leader

10 Hogan, R., Curphy, G. and Hogan, J., 'What We Know about Leadership', *American Psychologist* (June 1994), https://pdfs.semanticscholar.org/a705/2f29f15cb4c8c637f0d-c0b505793b37575d7.pdf

11 Mayo, Margarita, 'If Humble People Make the Best Leaders, Why Do We Fall for Charismatic Narcissists?', *Harvard Business Review*, 7 April 2017, https://hbr.org/2017/04/if-humble-people-make-the-best-leaders-why-do-we-fall-for-charismatic-narcissists

12 Zenger, Jack and Folkmann, Joseph, 'We Like Leaders Who Underrate Themselves', *Harvard Business Review*, 10

November 2015, https://hbr.org/2015/11/we-like-leaders-who-underrate-themselves

13 https://www.wired.com/2014/10/future-of-artificial-intelligence/

14 Prime, J. and Salib, E., 'the Best Leaders are Humble Leaders', *Harvard Business Review* (2014), https://hbr.org/2014/05/the-best-leaders-are-humble-leaders?referral=03758&cm_vc=rr_item_page.top_right

14 http://interactauthentically.com/articles/research/top-complaints-employees/

15 Schmidt, Eric and Rosenberg, Jonathan, *How Google Works* (2015), John Murray Press

16 https://www.fastcompany.com/3037542/productivity-hack-of-the-week-the-two-pizza-approach-to-productive-teamwork

17 Hill, L. and Kent, L., 'Good Managers Lead Through a Team', *Harvard Business Review*, 3 April 2012, https://hbr.org/2012/04/good-managers-lead-through-a-t

18 Reynolds, A. and Lewis, D., 'Teams Solve Problems Faster When They're More Cognitively Diverse', *Harvard Business Review*, 30 March 2017, https://hbr.org/2017/03/teams-solve-problems-faster-when-theyre-more-cognitively-diverse

CULTURE

1 'The Word's Broken Workplace', 13 June 2017, http://www.gallup.com/opinion/chairman/212045/world-broken-workplace.aspx?g_source=EMPLOYEE_ENGAGEMENT&g_medium=topic&g_campaign=tiles

2 https://www.adp.com/boost/articles/the-value-of-human-capital-measuring-your-most-important-assets-13-574

3 See the pioneering work of Baruch Lev, an accounting professor in the United States who has sought to establish new accounting principles to ensure that the true value of intangible assets is more fully captured in the official accounts of publicly listed corporations.

4 http://www.smartcompany.com.au/people-human-resources/managing/the-increasing-importance-of-intangible-assets/

5 http://uk.sodexo.com/files/live/sites/sdxcom-uk/files/050C_Country.com_UK_(English)/Building_Blocks/LOCAL/Multimedia/PDF/Press_Releases/2016/Knowledge-workers-research.pdf

6 http://www.nesta.org.uk/publications/uk-investment-intangible-assets

7 Hess, E. and Ludwig, K. (2017) *Humility is the New Smart: Rethinking Human Excellence in the Smart Machine* Age, McGraw-Hill Education

8 See https://www.shrm.org/hr-today/news/hr-magazine/0616/pages/using-algorithms-to-build-a-better-workforce.aspx; https://onstrategyhq.com/resources/googles-approach-to-employee-engagement-surprise-its-an-algorithm/; and https://www.wsj.com/articles/in-unilevers-radical-hiring-experiment-resumes-are-out-algorithms-are-in-1498478400

9 Ford, Martin (2015) *The Rise of the Robots: Technology and the Threat of Mass Unemployment*, Oneworld

10 Frey, C. and Osborn, M. (2013) 'The Future of Employment: How Susceptible are Jobs to Computerisation', http://www.oxfordmartin.ox.ac.uk/downloads/academic/The_Future_of_Employment.pdf

11 OECD, 'The Risk of Automation for Jobs in OECD Countries', working paper (2016), http://www.oecd-ilibrary.org/docserver/download/5jlz9h56dvq7-en.pdf?expires=1499092791&id=id&accname=guest&checksum=F29B1BB4462FAB88473176EBB688FFB8

12 Smith, David, 'Why Fear the March of the Robots? We will be walking hand in hand', *The Times*, 19 April 2017, https://www.thetimes.co.uk/article/why-fear-the-march-of-the-robots-we-will-be-walking-hand-in-hand-hcjnbl7bt

13 http://www.pbs.org/newshour/bb/second-machine-age-will-require-more-human-creativity/

14 'The Three Breakthroughs that have finally unleashed AI on the World', *Wired* (2014), https://www.wired.com/2014/10/future-of-artificial-intelligence/

15 Gartner (2016), 'Top Strategic Predictions for 2017 and Beyond: Surviving the Storm Winds of Digital Disruption', http://www.gartner.com/binaries/content/assets/events/keywords/cio/ciode5/top_strategic_predictions_fo_315910.pdf

16 https://hbr.org/2017/04/what-will-happen-when-your-companys-algorithms-go-wrong

17 O'Neil, Cathy (2016) *Weapons of Math Destruction: How Big Data Increases Inequality and Threatens Democracy*, Penguin

18 'The Three Breakthroughs', *Wired*, op cit

19 http://www.marginalia.online/humility-the-key-to-success-in-the-smart-machine-age/

20 http://www2.cipd.co.uk/pm/peoplemanagement/b/weblog/archive/2015/04/17/how-to-stop-office-banter-becoming-serious-sexual-harassment.aspx

21 Donald Clifton, the former educational psychologist who founded Gallup and developed the Q12 survey, insisted on measuring workplace friendships for good reason; it's one of the strongest predictors of productivity. Studies show that employees with a best friend at work tend to be more focused, more passionate and more loyal to their organizations. They get sick less often, suffer fewer accidents and change jobs less frequently. They even have more satisfied customers. See Ron Friedman's 2014 article in *New York* magazine, 'You Need a Work Best Friend', http://nymag.com/scienceofus/2014/12/you-need-a-work-best-friend.html

22 https://blogs.wsj.com/atwork/2015/04/02/what-do-workers-want-from-the-boss/?mod=e2tw&utm_source=huffingtonpost.
com&utm_medium=referral&utm_campaign=pubexchange_article

23 http://www.huffingtonpost.com/entry/bad-boss-mental-health_us_5873b3fee4b043ad97e4a444

24 Goffee, R. and Jones, G. (2015), *Why Should Anyone Work Here? What it Takes to Create an Authentic Organisation*, Harvard Business Review Press; for New York Life see https://www.newyorklife.com/about/our-strength/

25 https://hbr.org/2015/03/how-to-finally-kill-the-useless-recurring-meeting

26 Schmidt and Rosenberg, *How Google Works*, op cit

27 https://hbr.org/2014/01/how-netflix-reinvented-hr

28 http://www.condecosoftware.com/uk/products/workspace-occupancy-sensor

29 http://www.pcworld.com/article/2158204/10-tools-for-stealthily-slacking-off-at-work.html

30 https://www.tinypulse.com/blog/dw-why-remote-workers-are-happier-than-everyone-else-new-report

Also worth reading are the following *Harvard Business Review* articles:

Daniel Goleman, 'Leadership that Gets Results' (March–April 2000) and 'What Makes a Leader?' (January 2004); Robert Goffee and Gareth Jones, 'Why Should Anyone Be Led by You?' (Sep–Oct 2000); Jim Collins, 'Level 5 Leadership: The Triumph of Humility and Fierce Resolve' (July–Aug 2005); W. C. H. Prentice, 'Understanding Leadership' (Jan 2004); Hermina Ibarra, 'The Authenticity Paradox' (March 2016); Lisa Rosh and Lynn Offermann, 'Be Yourself – but Carefully' (Oct 2013); Jeanine Prime and Elizabeth Salib, 'The Best Leaders are Humble Leaders' (2014).

See also Erik Brynjolfsson and Andrew McAfee, *The Second Machine Age: Work, Progress and Prosperity in a Time of Brilliant Technologies* (2014), W.W. Norton.

CASH

1   http://www.aatcomment.org.uk/why-financial-literacy-is-es-sential-for-the-next-generation-of-entrepreneurs/
2   Davidson, S. (1994) *The Language of Business*, Thomas Horton & Daughters
3   Geijsbeek, J. B. (1914) *Ancient Double Entry Booking: Luca Pacioli's Treatise*
4   Woods, F. and Robinson, S. (2004) *Book-Keeping and Accounting*, FT Prentice Hall, p. 26
5   Ibid., p. 8

CONVERSATION

1   https://www.freeman.com/resources/brand-experience-a-new-era-in-marketing#c
2   https://www2.deloitte.com/us/en/pages/technology-me-dia-and-telecommunications/articles/digital-democracy-survey-generational-media-consump-tion-trends.html
3   See Tapscott, D. and Williams, A. D. (2006) *Wikinomics: How Mass Collaboration Changes Everything*, Atlantic Books
4   Thomas L. Friedman, in his recent book *The World is Flat*, identified the rise of what he calls the 'uploading revolution', in which a wide range of individually and community created information is made available via the internet, as one of his seven key forces 'flattening the world', and in his view the most disruptive of all of them. For Friedman, one of the most important aspects of this capacity to upload is that it is not merely isolated individuals putting their content on the web, but ad hoc communities which form and self-organize to create and self-regulate the quality of the content.
5   Leadbeater, C. (2007) *We-Think: Mass Innovation, Not Mass Production*, Profile Books

6 Godin, Seth (2006) *Small is the New Big*, Penguin

7 See Jaffe, Joseph (2007) *Join the Conversation: How to Engage Marketing-Weary Consumers with the Power of Community, Dialogue, and Partnership*, John Wiley & Sons, p. 1

8 Godin, Seth (2007) *Meatball Sundae: How New Marketing Is Transforming the Business World*, Piatkus Books

9 Zeldin, T. (2000) *Conversation: How Talk Can Change Our Lives*, Hidden Spring

10 McCarthy, E. J. (1981) *Basic Marketing: A Managerial Approach*, Richard D. Irwin

11 Mercer, David (1995) *Marketing*, second edition, Wiley Blackwell, p. 29

12 Ibid., p. 30

13 For example, Booms and Bitner added another three Ps to the traditional Four Ps to make them more relevant for the service sector. Their three Ps were: *People* – people often are the service itself. *Process* – how the service is delivered to the consumer is frequently an important part of the service. *Physical evidence* – the context in which products and services are purchased, which is considered by some to be part of the product package. See Booms, B. H. and Bitner, M. J. (1981) *Marketing Strategies and Organization Structures for Service Firms*, Marketing of Services, Donnelly, J. and George, W. R. (eds), American Marketing Association

14 https://www.freeman.com/resources/brand-experience-a-new-era-in-marketing#c

15 'Brand Experience: A New Era in Marketing: New Data from the 2017 Freeman Global Brand Experience Survey', https://www.freeman.com/resources/brand-experience-a-new-era-in-marketing#c

16 See e.g. http://puzzlelondonsport.com/red-bulls-success-spon-sorship/; https://www.ama.org/resources/Pages/red-bull-wings-creating-successful-marketing-oriented-or-ganization.aspx; and http://linkhumans.com/blog/red-bull

17 http://www.oceanroadmedia.co.uk/blog/branding/a-lesson-in-branding-and-content-marketing-from-red-bull/

18 http://puzzlelondonsport.com/red-bulls-success-sponsorship/

19 http://www.beveragedaily.com/Markets/The-world-s-unquenchable-thirst-for-energy-drinks

20 https://www.redbullmediahouse.com

21 https://www.redbullmediahouse.com/products/mobile/
     red-bull-mobile.html

22 https://www.linkedin.com/pulse/75-marketers-have-wrong-
     idea-content-john-hall

23 See Jaffe, Joseph (2007) *Join the Conversation: How to
     Engage Marketing-Weary Consumers with the Power of
     Community, Dialogue, and Partnership*, John Wiley &
     Sons, p. 6

24 Kotler, Philip et al., *Marketing 4.0: Moving from Traditional
     to Digital* (2016), Wiley

25 Ibid

26 https://hbr.org/2013/11/make-the-most-of-a-polarizing-brand

27 http://www.independent.co.uk/travel/news-and-advice/
     ryanair-may-charge-a-fat-taxrsquo-for-its-overweight-passen-
     gers-1672979.html

28 The term *prosumer* was originally coined by the futurologist
     Alvin Toffler (see Toffler, A., 1980, *The Third Wave*, Pan
     Books), and has since been modified and used by other writers.
     Tapscott and Williams recently elaborated on the related
     phrase 'prosumption' (production/consumption) to refer to
     the process in which consumers are increasingly participating
     in the creation of products in an active and ongoing way (see
     Tapscott and Williams, 2006, *Wikinomics: How Mass
     Collaboration Changes Everything*, Atlantic Books, p.126)

29 http://www.dmnews.com/content-marketing/10-stats-that-
     show-why-user-generated-content-works/article/444872/

30 http://www.adweek.com/digital/sxsw-millennials-trust-us-
     er-generated-content-50-traditional-media/

31 Bonchek, Mark and France, Cara, 'What Creativity in
     Marketing Looks Like Today', *Harvard Business Review*,
     22 March 2017

32 Leadbeater, C. (2008) *We-Think: Mass Innovation, Not
     Mass Production*, Profile Books, p.100

33 https://hbr.org/visual-library/2014/12/the-participation-scale

34 https://ideas.lego.com/dashboard; also see https://www.
     visioncritical.com/5-examples-how-brands-are-using-co-crea-
     tion/

35 https://ideas.lego.com/projects/35dacd9d-fb79-4048-a39f-
     199d56d8a8eb

36 https://www.youtube.com/watch?v=t2XFh_tD2RA

37 Fleit, Caren (2017) *The Evolution of the Chief Marketing
     Officer*, Harvard Business Press

38 http://www.zdnet.com/article/retailer-or-a-data-company-wal-mart-is-now-both/]

39 http://www.walmartlabs.com

40 http://www.huffingtonpost.com/al-norman/the-walmartface-book-socia_b_1714802.html

41 https://www.dezyre.com/article/how-big-data-analysis-helped-increase-walmarts-sales-turnover/109]

42 http://www.fusioncharts.com/blog/2014/03/how-walmart-us-es-data-visualization-to-convert-real-time-social-conversa-tions-into-inventory/

43 https://hbr.org/2015/07/your-company-should-be-helping-customers-on-social

44 http://www.socialmediaexaminer.com/8-ways-to-use-social-listening-for-your-business/

45 https://hbr.org/2015/07/your-company-should-be-helping-customers-on-social

46 https://www2.deloitte.com/content/dam/Deloitte/ch/Documents/consumer-business/ch-en-consumer-busi-ness-made-to-order-consumer-review.pdf

47 https://www.theguardian.com/facebook-partner-zone/2016/may/20/the-importance-of-social-media-listening

48 Godin, Seth (2007) *Meatball Sundae: How New Marketing Is Transforming the Business World*, Piatkus Books, p.77

49 McClure, Samuel M. et al., 'Neural Correlates of Behavioural Preference for Culturally Familiar Drinks', *Neuron* 44(2) (2004), pp. 379–87

50 http://www.newneuromarketing.com/5-neuromarketing-tech-niques-every-marketer-should-know-about

Also worth reading:

The classic marketing text is, of course, Philip Kotler's *Marketing Management*, with the thirteenth edition having been published in 2008, and it remains the most widely used text in graduate business schools. There are a raft of new marketing theorists worth reading. For example, Seth Godin's work is incisive and fun, as is Joseph Jaffe's brilliant book *Join the Conversation*. Locke and colleagues' book *The Cluetrain Manifesto* is also an important backdrop to this section – it popularized the idea that markets are socially constructed and should be thought of as conversations.

The segment on the Five Cs was also inspired by a number of contemporary accounts of personalization and customization.

For example, the Lego MINDSTORMS® Robot example is featured in *Wikinomics*, Tapscott and Williams's essential account of how they believe the rise of mass collaboration changes everything. Charles Leadbeater's book eloquently covers similar territory.

SOCIAL MEDIA MARKETING RESOURCES

It's self-evident that *The 80 Minute MBA* can't be a comprehensive 'how to' guide – it's aim is to get you to think broadly about the task of leading and managing successful businesses. The rapid growth in social media poses particular challenges in terms of where to direct you for advice. A quick google.co.uk search returns 66 million results alone for 'social media marketing tips'.

Below are some good general sources and interesting articles:

https://www.socialbakers.com (subscription required but a useful source of up to date social media marketing stats globally)

https://blog.hootsuite.com/social-listening-business/

http://www.toptenreviews.com/services/internet/best-social-media-monitoring/

https://www.socialbakers.com/blog/2661-the-ethical-dilemma-should-companies-take-sides

Quesenberry, K. A., 'Fix Your Social Media Strategy by Taking it Back to Basics', *Harvard Business Review*, 25 July 2016

Benmark, G. and Singer, D., 'Turn Customer Care into "Social Care" to Break Away from the Competition', *Harvard Business Review*, 19 December 2012

'The Trouble with CMOs', *Harvard Business Review* (July–August 2017)

Power, B., 'How AI is Streamlining Marketing and Sales', *Harvard Business Review*, 12 June 2017

Nichols, W., 'Advertising Analytics 2.0', *Harvard Business Review* (March 2013)

Finally, the 30-second advertising slot isn't dead, but it works best in blockbuster content, where the guaranteed eyes-on audience have kept the cost of securing those costs high, driving higher production costs for adverts that feature in those slots, the Super Bowl in the US being one of the best examples: see http://fortune.com/2017/01/30/super-bowl-commercials-marketing/

PICTURE CREDITS

We would like to thank the following for kindly supplying material for use in this book:

THE 80 MINUTE MBA LIVE!

80 Minute MBA live events are run exclusively through The London Business Forum. In these fun, high-impact sessions, Richard Reeves and John Knell bring the content of this book to life.

For more information or to book places, go to www.londonbusinessforum.com, call 020 7600 4222, or email info@londonbusinessforum.com.

THE 80 MINUTE MBA WITHIN YOUR ORGANIZATION

Is your company in need of some inspiration? If so, Richard and John can be booked to run *The 80 Minute MBA* event within your organization.

To check their availability and costs call The London Business Forum on 020 7600 4222 or email info@londonbusinessforum.com.

HORRiD HENRY
Tricks and Treats

HORRiD HENRY
Tricks and
Treats

Francesca Simon
Illustrated by Tony Ross

Orion
Children's Books

Horrid Henry Tricks and Treats originally appeared in
Horrid Henry and the Bogey Babysitter first published in Great Britain in
2002 by Orion Children's Books
This edition first published in Great Britain in 2011
by Orion Children's Books
a division of the Orion Publishing Group Ltd
Orion House
5 Upper Saint Martin's Lane
London WC2H 9EA
An Hachette UK Company

7 9 10 8 6

A catalogue record for this book is available from the British Library.

ISBN 978 1 4440 0109 9

Printed in China.

www.orionbooks.co.uk
www.horridhenry.co.uk

For the divine
Alice Burden

There are many more **Horrid Henry** books
available. For a complete list visit
www.horridhenry.co.uk
or
www.orionbooks.co.uk

Contents

Chapter 1

Hallowe'en!
Oh happy, happy day!

Every year Horrid Henry could
not believe it: an entire day devoted
to stuffing your face with sweets
and playing horrid tricks. Best of all,
you were *supposed* to stuff your face
and play horrid tricks.

Whoopee!

Horrid Henry was armed and ready.
He had loo roll.
He had water pistols.
He had shaving foam.
Oh my, would he be playing
tricks tonight.

Anyone who didn't instantly
hand over a fistful of sweets
would get it with the foam.

And **woe betide** any fool
who gave him an apple.
Horrid Henry knew how to treat
rotten grown-ups like that.

His red and black devil costume
lay ready on the bed, complete
with evil mask, twinkling horns,
trident, and whippy tail.
He'd scare everyone wearing that.
"Heh heh heh," said Horrid Henry,
practising his evil laugh.

"Henry," came a little voice outside his bedroom door, "come and see my new costume."

"No," said Henry. "I'm busy."

16

"You're just jealous because *my* costume is nicer than yours," said Peter.

"Am not."

"Are too."

Come to think of it, what *was* Peter wearing?

Last year he'd copied Henry's
monster costume and ruined
Henry's Hallowe'en.

What if he were copying Henry's
devil costume? That would be just
like that horrible little copycat.
"All right, you can come in for
two seconds," said Henry.

A big, pink, bouncy bunny
bounded into Henry's room.
It had little white bunny ears.
It had a little white bunny tail.
It had pink polka dots
everywhere else.

Horrid Henry groaned.
What a stupid costume.
Thank goodness he wasn't
wearing it.

"Isn't it great?" said Perfect Peter.

"No," said Henry. "It's horrible."

"You're just saying that to
be mean, Henry," said Peter,
bouncing up and down.
"I can't wait to go trick-or-treating
in it tonight."

Chapter 2

Oh no.

Horrid Henry felt as if he'd been punched in the stomach.

Henry would be expected to go out
trick-or-treating . . . with Peter!
He, Henry, would have to walk
around with a pink polka dot bunny.
Everyone would see him.
The shame of it!

Rude Ralph would never stop
teasing him. Moody Margaret
would call him a bunny wunny.
How could he play tricks on people
with a pink polka dot bunny
following him everywhere?
He was ruined.
His name would be a joke.

"You can't wear that,"
said Henry desperately.

"Yes I can," said Peter.

"I won't let you," said Henry.

Perfect Peter looked at Henry.
"You're just jealous."

Grrr!

Horrid Henry was about to tear
that stupid costume off Peter when,
suddenly, he had an idea.

It was painful.
It was humiliating.

But anything was better than having
Peter prancing about in pink
polka dots.

Chapter 3

"Tell you what," said Henry,
"just because I'm so nice I'll let you
borrow my monster costume.
You've always wanted to wear it."

"NO!" said Peter.
"I want to be a bunny."

"But you're supposed to be scary for
Hallowe'en," said Henry.

"I am scary," said Peter.
"I'm going to bounce up to people
and yell 'boo'."

"I can make you really scary, Peter,"
said Horrid Henry.

"How?" said Peter.

"Sit down and I'll show you."
Henry patted his desk chair.

"What are you going to do?"
said Peter suspiciously.
He took a step back.

"Nothing," said Henry.
"I'm just trying to help you."

Perfect Peter didn't move.
"How can I be scarier?"
he said cautiously.

"I can give you a scary haircut,"
said Henry.

Perfect Peter clutched his curls.
"But I like my hair," he said feebly.

"This is Hallowe'en," said Henry.
"Do you want to be scary
or don't you?"

"Um, um, uh," said Peter,
as Henry pushed him down in
the chair and got out the scissors.

"Not too much," squealed Peter.

"Of course not," said Horrid Henry.
"Just sit back and relax,
I promise you'll love this."

Horrid Henry twirled the scissors.

Snip! Snip! Snip!

Snip! Snip!

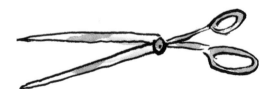

Chapter 4

Magnificent, thought Horrid Henry.
He gazed proudly at his work.

Maybe he should be a hairdresser when he grew up. Yes! Henry could see it now. Customers would queue for miles for one of Monsieur Henri's scary snips.

Shame his genius was wasted on someone as yucky as Peter. Still . . .

"You look great, Peter," said Henry.
"Really scary. Atomic Bunny.
Go and have a look."

Peter went over and looked
in the mirror.

"AAAAAAAAAARGGGGGGG!"

"Scared yourself, did you?"
said Henry. "That's great."

"AAAAAAAAAARGGGGGGG!"

howled Peter.

Mum ran into the room.

"AAAAAAAAAARGGGGGGG!"

howled Mum.

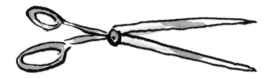

"AAAAAAAAAARGGGGGGG!"

howled Peter.

"Henry!" screeched Mum.
"What have you done?!
You horrid, horrid boy!"

What was left of Peter's hair stuck up in **ragged** tufts all over his head.

On one side was a
big bald patch.

"I was just making him look scary," protested Henry. "He said I could."

"Henry made me!" said Peter.

"My poor baby," said Mum. She glared at Henry.

"No trick-or-treating for you," said Mum. "You'll stay here."

Horrid Henry could hardly believe his ears. This was the worst thing that had ever happened to him.

"NO!"

howled Henry.
This was all Peter's fault.
"I hate you, Peter!" he screeched.

Then he attacked.
He was Medusa, coiling round
her victim with her snaky hair.

"Aaaahh!"

screeched Peter.

"Henry!" shouted Mum.
"Go to your room!"

Chapter 5

Mum and Peter left the house to go trick-or-treating.

Henry had screamed and sobbed and begged. He'd put on his devil costume, just in case his tears melted their stony hearts.

But no.

His mean, horrible parents
wouldn't change their mind.
Well, they'd be sorry.
They'd all be sorry.

Dad came into the sitting room.
He was holding a large shopping bag.
"Henry, I've got some work to finish
so I'm going to let you hand out
treats to any trick-or-treaters."

Horrid Henry stopped plotting
his revenge. Had Dad gone mad?
Hand out treats?
What kind of punishment was this?
Horrid Henry fought to keep
a big smile off his face.

"Here's the Hallowe'en stuff,
Henry," said Dad.
He handed Henry the heavy bag.
"But remember," he added sternly,
"these treats are not for you:
they're to give away."

Yeah, right,

thought Henry.

"OK, Dad," he said as meekly
as he could. "Whatever you say."
Dad went back to the kitchen.

Now was his chance!
Horrid Henry leapt on the bag.
Wow, was it full! He'd grab all the
good stuff, throw back anything
yucky with lime or peppermint,
and he'd have enough sweets to keep
him going for at least a week!

Henry yanked open the bag.
A terrible sight met his eyes.

The bag was full of satsumas.
And apples.
And walnuts in their shells.

No wonder his horrible parents
had trusted him to be in charge of it.

Ding dong.

Slowly, Horrid Henry heaved his
heavy bones to the door.
There was his empty, useless trick-
or-treat bag, sitting forlornly by the
entrance. Henry gave it a kick,
then opened the door and glared.

"Whaddya want?"
snapped Horrid Henry.

"Trick or treat,"
whispered Weepy William.
He was dressed as a pirate.

Horrid Henry held out
the bag of horrors.
"Lucky dip!" he announced.
"Close your eyes for a big surprise!"
William certainly would be surprised
at what a rotten treat he'd be getting.

Weepy William put down
his swag bag, closed his eyes tight,
then plunged his hand into
Henry's lucky dip.
He rummaged and he rummaged
and he rummaged, hoping to find
something better than satsumas.

Horrid Henry eyed Weepy William's
bulging swag bag.

Go on, Henry, urged the bag.
He'll never notice.

Horrid Henry did not wait
to be asked twice.

Dip!
Zip!
Pop!

Horrid Henry grabbed a big handful
of William's sweets and popped them
inside his empty bag.

Weepy William opened his eyes.
"Did you take some of my sweets?"

"No," said Henry.

William peeked inside his bag
and burst into tears.
"Waaaaaaaa!" wailed William.
"Henry took . . ."

Henry pushed him out
and slammed the door.

Dad came running.
"What's wrong?"

"Nothing," said Henry.
"Just William crying 'cause he's
scared of pumpkins."

Phew, thought Henry.
That was close. Perhaps he had been
a little too greedy.

Chapter 6

Ding dong.

It was Lazy Linda wearing
a pillowcase over her head.
Gorgeous Gurinder was with her,
dressed as a scarecrow.

"Trick or treat!"
"Trick or treat!"

"Close your eyes for a big surprise!"
said Henry, holding out
the lucky dip bag.

"Ooh, a lucky dip!" squealed Linda.

Lazy Linda and Gorgeous Gurinder
put down their bags, closed their
eyes, and reached into the lucky dip.

66

Lazy Linda opened her eyes. "You give the worst treats ever, Henry," said Linda, gazing at her walnut in disgust.

"We won't be coming back *here*," sniffed Gorgeous Gurinder.

Tee hee, thought Horrid Henry.

Ding dong.

It was Beefy Bert.
He was wearing a robot costume.

"Hi, Bert, got any good sweets?"
asked Henry.

"I dunno," said Beefy Bert.

Horrid Henry soon found out
that he did.

Lots and lots and lots
of them.

So did Moody Margaret,

Sour Susan,

Jolly Josh

and Tidy Ted.

Soon Henry's bag was stuffed
with treats.

Ding dong.

Horrid Henry opened the door.

"Boo," said Atomic Bunny.

Henry's sweet bag!
Help! Mum would see it!

"Eeeeek!"

screeched Horrid Henry.
"Help! Save me!"

Quickly, he ran upstairs
clutching his bag and hid it
safely under his bed.

Phew, that was close.

"Don't be scared, Henry,
it's only me," called Perfect Peter.

Horrid Henry came back downstairs.

"No!" said Henry.
"I'd never have known."

"Really?" said Peter.

"Really," said Henry.

"Everyone just gave sweets
this year," said Perfect Peter.

"Yuck."

Horrid Henry held out the lucky dip.

"Ooh, a satsuma," said Peter.
"Aren't I lucky?"

"I hope you've learned your lesson,
Henry," said Mum sternly.

"I certainly have,"
said Horrid Henry, eyeing
Perfect Peter's bulging bag.
"Good things come to those
who wait."